Liberal for
Conservative Reasons

- or -

*How to stop being obnoxious
and start winning elections.*

PETER RICE

A Dog Tooth Paperback
Albuquerque, New Mexico

Cover by Sam Covarrubias.

ISBN: 1544841485
ISBN-13: 978-1544841489

For my right-of-center friends: Dick, Katie, Chuck, Judy, Barry E., Barry W., Cris, Whitney, Lauren, Matt, and John. Because to the extent I speak Conservative, it is thanks to you, and because after this, you may be my only friends.

CONTENTS

"*A heart can no more be forced to love than a stomach can be forced to digest food by persuasion.*" —Alfred Nobel

"*We make out of the quarrel with others, rhetoric, but of the quarrel with ourselves, poetry.*" —William Butler Yeats

Chapter One

_____

A time to win: Why we should quit being liberal for the "right" reasons.

YOU MAY ASK YOURSELF: HOW DID WE GET HERE?

We, the great liberal tribe of all that is right and just and fair (allegedly), did not expect to be rounding out the 2010s watching a reality-TV-star-turned-president appoint cabinet members based mostly on their convictions that the departments they sought to lead should cease to exist. We did not expect to be constantly on edge over the state of Ruth Bader Ginsburg's pulse. We did not expect to be crashing Canadian immigration FAQ sites. We did not expect to be a movement under siege, holed up in our big cities, a shell of our former political selves, going to the occasional protest march and awkwardly cheering on tired lions named Pelosi and Schumer.

We knew (*knew!*) that America's swelling ranks of enlightened or comfortable or non-white people would add up to a new center-left coalition that could grind the opposition into powder and force a reckoning – force them to repent for their immigrant bashing, for their tax cuts for the rich, for their perennial assault on Medicare and Social Security, and for their constant mispronunciation of the word "nuclear."

We knew that would happen because we knew the people agreed with us on the issues. Gun safety? Health care? Environmental protection? Legal abortion? Infrastructure spending? Progressive taxation? Minimum wage? College affordability? *We got this*. The people love it. All of it.

Most of all, we knew we would win because we had a firm command of the moral high ground. We stood with women, minorities, workers, and salamanders. We were on the right side of history, of justice, and of a gender-neutral God or divine force or whatever is cool with you, man. We all *knew* that those gun owners put themselves before the safety of kids, that healthcare is a human right, and that we had an obligation to stop the wholesale destruction of species after species whose habitats are being ploughed over to build more strip malls. Workers *deserve* to be able to live on a full-time minimum wage and send their kids to college – *it's the right thing to do*. Moral societies (insert allusion to some European country here) take care of their most vulnerable. *We* were right and *they* were deplorable.

And then, we got our asses handed to us by a crazy person.

Crow all you like about the popular vote. (It certainly helped me get through a couple of tough weeks.) But at the end of the day, we knew the rules, we played the game, and we got creamed. The least popular presidential candidate in modern history went into our backyard, found people who should have been with us, turned them, and ran away with it. Many of those voters quite reasonably found the candidate himself to be loathsome, but pulled the lever anyway.

And further down the ticket, the blue tide continued to recede. These days, you can invite all the Democratic governors over for a dinner party and use a studio apartment as the venue. Ten years ago, you would have needed at least a two bedroom affair with a patio, and the party itself would have been way more fun, if only because it would have included New Mexico's Bill Richardson. Republicans control 32 legislatures outright, and split control of another six. You can now take a road trip from Miami to Seattle without touching a state under total democratic control.

You might reasonably wonder if we're just a more conservative country than you thought. But if so, how do you explain this sample of recent polls: On global climate change, 59 percent of Americans say we're not doing enough to address it (Quinnipiac). On immigration, 60 percent favor allowing undocumented immigrants with jobs to become legal residents, and 71 percent say the government should not attempt mass deportations (CNN/ORC). Infrastructure: 90 percent think we should spend more money on it (Quinnipiac). Planned Parenthood: 58 percent oppose cutting off federal funding (Suffolk/USA Today). Drugs: 60 percent say marijuana should be legal (Gallup). Energy: 65 percent say focusing on solar and wind is more important than focusing on coal and natural gas (Bloomberg). Healthcare: 60 percent want to leave Obamacare as is *or change it so it does even more* (McClatchy-Marist). Trade: 60 percent say foreign exchange has either helped us or made no difference (NBC). Minimum wage: 58 percent want to see it at $15 per hour (Pew). Civil rights: 58 percent think same sex marriage should be legal (CBS), and 79 percent say prejudice against minority groups is a very or somewhat serious problem (Quinnipiac).

So, how the hell do we manage to win so much and still lose?

We can, of course, diagnose many reasons for this unpleasant state of affairs: False equivalencies in the media, the obsession with horse race politics rather than issues, echoes of the southern strategy, James Comey, too much special interest money in politics, complacency over incorrect poll numbers, the complicated gender-based reactions to our last candidate, and whatever really is the matter with Kansas. And speaking of states, I hear that Wisconsin and Michigan are *just lovely* in the summer and fall – so maybe consider visiting them (Hillary!).

My conservative brother-in-law has a label for this sort of excuse making: Loser talk.

Point to things you cannot change, at least not without a time machine and an alternate universe, and blame them for your predicament. Lash out at the stupidity of the opposition, belittle them, maybe burrow into the protective cocoon of a protest march, and generally rally around the flag. Then call it a cathartic day. Do whatever you have to do to avoid looking in the mirror, because if you do, you may just notice an unfortunate reality lurking behind the electoral failure: Liberals, at least the ones who talk the most, are super annoying.

Take any one of the most popular arguments of our time, and we liberals will almost inevitably pick the right side for the most annoying reasons possible. We're in favor of immigration (good start) because we desperately want to love and be loved by all the various and sundry peoples of the world and speak all their languages and try all their cuisines in a sensitive way that does not veer into cultural appropriation (annoying). We're in favor of universal health care (sensible) because healthcare is a human right and Denmark does it (annoying). And we're in favor of social welfare programs (smart) because if you can afford an $8 coffee, you can afford to help the homeless (annoying).

Meanwhile, a giant segment of lefty politics seems to have abandoned the policy front altogether in favor of an unfocused and itinerant airing of grievances (always super annoying). They occupied Wall Street for a while, because apparently camping on something will change it for the better. But attention soon shifted to the important business of writing trigger warnings, and later, the Bernie Sanders campaign (a few points here for some semblance of an actual agenda). After that ended, the emotional energy was diverted to a grand attempt at reversing our nation's troubled history with Native Americans and the environment by drafting sensible omnibus legislation strengthening tribal sovereignty and environmental regulation. I'm just kidding of course. They actually camped out at a pipeline for a while.

But it's all good. Nothing much important was happening in the summer and fall of 2016 that could have used a little more attention.

In the process of being so obnoxious, liberals turn themselves into targets. For every sob story about some poor soul on welfare, every self-congratulatory discussion about the benefits of diversity, and every camping trip/protest, we come off as holier-than-thou or out of touch or just plain weird. The moral arguments we make reduce our voting bloc to a core group that usually does not constitute a majority. And our intellectual arguments, usually inserted into deeply emotional or instinctual disputes, cement our political isolation.

Conservative politicians need only pick these political weapons of war up off the ground and use them against us. They then run on a carefully planned platform of not being anything like those strange and annoying city folk on their high horses who give every impression of hating you. You, the welder in Oklahoma City who favors liberal dispensation of healthcare and progressive taxation but votes Republican because you do not appreciate being thought of as evil over a few hangups about gender-neutral bathrooms.

And here, perhaps, it would be appropriate to establish my liberal credentials, lest I be tarnished as a Manchurian hack: I grew up in Olympia, Washington, a place where the real political controversy comes between the Democrats (right wing sellouts!) and the Greens or whatever fringe lefty third party is in vogue lately. I went to a (liberal) liberal arts college, spent a few years as a newspaper reporter (elitist *and* liberal), and my presidential voting track records includes not a single Republican. I am currently writing this from a Starbucks in downtown Buenos Aires, where I ordered, in a big scary foreign language, a venti English breakfast tea that happily remains close at hand. Yes, dear reader, *I am too liberal even for coffee.* I don't even own a car.

And yet, I flatter myself into thinking that at least I am not annoying about it, and a not-very-scientific poll of my closest conservative friends would confirm this. They often say things like, "I disagree with you but at least you're thoughtful." (Thanks, guys!) One conservative friend, upon hearing some reasonable liberal thing I've said, often insists that I'm actually a conservative.

For a while, I thought that friend might have a point. Maybe somewhere between the cracks of supporting universal health care, food stamps, and strong workplace safety regulation, there was actually a bubbling well of conservative ooze rising and threatening to submerge the whole commie thought paradigm. Perhaps I would soon take out a subscription to *Cigar Aficionado,* join a country club, and start ranting about the takers all the time. Perhaps this was all just a normal process of getting older, like getting up earlier, increased instances of nose hair maintenance, or bafflement over what the millennials are up to lately.

This was a genuinely fun possibility to entertain, because transgressive behavior is always alluring, especially when it offends liberals. Yet this brilliant idea kept getting thwarted by my actual opinions on actual issues. The devil-may-care attitude of conservative politicians may be refreshing sometimes, but their positions are super problematic, to say the least.

Over time, I've come to the conclusion that this supposed reasonableness that my conservative friends see isn't terribly complicated: It's just a near-total lack of moral sanctimony. They can talk to me, often late into the night, about all manner of politics, but they won't hear a lot of claptrap about safe spaces, privilege, or the words engraved on the Statue of Liberty. I'll proudly carry the lefty flag, just not with those particular trappings they find so annoying. I will think those thoughts, of course, but on my better days they stay in my head.

(If you don't believe me, and wish to personally verify the existence of my morality-based bleeding heart, then the next time you're in Albuquerque you should buy me a stiff drink and ask me about voter ID laws.)

There's an important strategic reasons for this, of course: I wish to remain friends with these people. My conservative buddies all seem to have nice houses with comfortable patios, and they enjoy drinking margaritas on hot summer nights, which is reason enough to avoid annoying them with moral sanctimony.

But more to the point, it's simply not necessary. There are perfectly good reasons to enact liberal policies that have nothing to do with what's "right" in a conventional liberal moral sense. Speaking a language of lefty morality is automatically divisive, since moderates, conservatives and not a few liberals don't relate to it. But speaking a language of practical causes and effects has at least the potential to transcend group identity politics. It's basic sales: Zero in on what your audience is interested in, not on what you're interested in.

But lest I get on a moral high horse about not moralizing, let me quickly point out that it's not all canny salesmanship in the pursuit of margaritas. I'm also lazy, cynical, and totally incapable of sustaining the kind of long-term outrage that so much of liberalism seems to be founded on. In short, I'm normal.

The people whose thoughts animate the left are deeply concerned about values like justice and equality. They see women making less money, poor people without enough to eat, or some ice sheet breaking off of Antarctica, and they quickly develop a deep sense of guilty panic about the whole state of affairs. On the public policy front, this can occasionally translate into slam dunk legislation like the Voting Rights Act or Medicare. But on a personal front, it can lead to some obsessive, puritanical, and generally annoying behavior, such as a religious devotion to organic food, excessive fretting about whether old credit cards can be recycled, the purchase of hybrid cars or Subarus, long stories about the 1960s, conspicuous use of hypothetical feminine gender pronouns, and an expectation that you too will follow them down this bizzare, twisting road.

Hanging out with people like that is very stressful, because everything you say or do could be a violation of some important rule. It's like adapting to the norms of a foreign country, except screw-ups bring moral castigation of an almost religious character, rather than a quiet and forgiving chuckle about the blundering foreigner who thought it was okay to own a Ford Excursion or shop at Wal-Mart.

This morality trip is to be expected from the side that is forever concerned with justice and equality, and it's not even an especially bad trait, at least in the abstract. The trouble is this: The world can be a pretty rough place, and not at all fair. So there is always a fresh cause to embrace, a new, softer, ever-more-hyphenated term to apply to maligned groups, or something else entirely, large or small, that you must feel empathy for or care deeply about or boycott, if only to telegraph to your fellows that you are one of the good people. You can't ever escape it, and it gets tiresome fast.

This is, to use a term all liberals can understand, unsustainable. People do not want to get out of bed in the morning only to have the yoke of imperialism, colonialism, sexism, racism, poverty, injustice, environmental destruction, and that coup in Guatemala placed on their shoulders. They especially do not want to have to lighten the burden via the purchase of psychological indulgences like a $7 orange at Whole Foods. They do not want to worry about the implications of eating a Chiquita banana (see the Guatemalan coup), or indulging in a delicious lunch at Chick-fil-A, or *driving a car*. Rather than cart a tin can all over town in search of a recycling depository, they would like to just throw the damn thing in the trash and be done with it. These people include myself.

At least one major social institution manages to get away with the tiresome repetition that "all have sinned and fallen short of the glory of God," but they are also hemorrhaging members despite the clutch selling point of eternal salvation. The same total bummer of a trope from a political movement isn't likely to fare much better. At best, I'll still schlep to the polls and vote for annoying over crazy, but it'll get lonlier every time. That lack of enthusiasm does not electoral majorities make.

Life is hard, and only a small percentage of Americans can actually hold that much empathetic feeling and moral posturing in their heads before burning out entirely and rebelling against it. If your political movement's first impression is a bunch of sanctimonious loser talk and conspicuous consumption in the form of urban elite moral peacocking (farmers markets, the Prius), then odds are good you will not get a chance to make a second impression with your great ideas about alternative energy and universal background checks. You eventually become so annoying that people vote for crazy instead.

I don't mean to diminish the real problems with our media, gerrymandering, Vladimir Putin, race, the natural pendulum swings of election cycles, and a thousand other things. But just for a moment imagine what political life would be like if the left didn't just have good ideas, but also had good style. Something open and inviting that did not ask you to immediately repent for your sins and those of your forefathers. What if it was okay to just say "forefathers" and not "foreparents?" What if we chilled out on the morality and focused on making sensible policy for everybody? What if we played offense for once, using arguments that appealed to more than just the base?

What if, in short, we stopped being liberal for the "right" reasons, and started being liberal for conservative reasons? Because conservatives, on their good days, are skeptical, sensible, and not afraid to hurt some feelings when called for. They are the ones that look wild new ideas in the face with a refreshing, unimpressed squint, and say things like "that sounds expensive." They are the people who point out obnoxious realities that we would prefer not to think about. They come off as relaxed and assured, possibly from the lack of hand wringing over every injustice the world has ever produced. They have many, many problems, especially with nearly every policy they advocate, but on their best days (and I fully concede they have not had too many lately), I really like the cut of their jib.

And that is no trivial point. Politicians project attitude and personality with everything they do, because they know politics is a much more instinctual game than anybody would like to admit. We sneered at this reality in 2000, because it's dumb to choose the leader of the free world based on how much you'd like to have a beer with a reformed alcoholic, but we were pretty happy when the spiritual intangibles in Obama's personality practically levitated people into the voting booth. We all spew out a lot of cheap talk about the importance of issues and policies and the Senate Foreign Relations Committee, and when discussing some new romantic fling we also talk about their nice personality and intellectual depth. But in both situations, we all know there's way more to it than that.

The guys who have actually taken up residence in the White House in recent years know that politics is a fundamentally emotional business, not some rational exercise based on enlightenment principles. They know that if you want to learn politics, you would probably do better watching a Jane Goodall documentary about chimpanzees than anything produced by CNN. They know that communicating policy arguments is important, but mostly because it works to sell a larger personality that knows where you're coming from on a gut level, has your back, and if need be, will not hesitate to send Seal Team Six over to the next valley to teach that other band of chimps what's what.

Being liberal for conservative reasons is part sales job and part enlightenment exercise, but mostly it's about that personality projection. Plenty of people out there are liberals but just don't know it yet, often because we have written them off as unsophisticated, immoral, deplorable, ignorant, racist or lacking compassion. But if we can argue a liberal policy agenda in a way that acknowledges the reality they live in and where they're coming from, we can demonstrate that we've got their backs. Do that, and perhaps one day in the not-too-distant future, one of the higher primates from our tribe will again get to ride around in a heavily fortified 747 called Air Force One.

But what does "liberal for conservative reasons" actually look like? We'll extrapolate it out, using this year's staple issues, in future chapters. But for now, by way of one taste of an example, let's take a deeper dive into one of my liberal credentials from above: The refusal to own a car.

Since I'm liberal and lives in the middle of an urban center, you probably assume that my not owning a car and getting around on a bicycle has to do with some moralistic reasoning, such as not wishing to support the brutal regime in Saudi Arabia or a general dislike of the carbon emissions that contribute to global warming. Or maybe I want to avoid jacking up demand for further asphalt-based development that contributes to the urban heat island effect (nerd points!).

Naturally, I abhor the Saudi regime and do not wish to contribute to carbon pollution, but using that morality play as the basis for not having a car quickly leads to some very tough and tiresome questions that don't seem productive to ask. If driving a car is wrong, then what is one supposed to do with friends who drive them? Are you obligated to never get into one of their cars? Or any car at all? What about the bus, which also uses fossil fuels and pollutes the atmosphere? What about Uber? If carbon pollution is the problem, then are you obligated to become a vegetarian, since cow farts are a shockingly large contributor to the climate change problem? Why not kick it up a notch and become a vegan? Are you obligated to not have kids, since people in general are basically carbon producing machines? For that matter, should you just do Mother Nature a solid and kill yourself right here and now?

And so it gets crazier and crazier, as morality plays often do. Soon you're spending a lot of time wondering how long you can kiss your girlfriend before it becomes a mortal sin, or whether switching on a light counts as starting a fire for sabbath observation purposes, or whether to buy local or organic if it's not possible to do both.

If morality is your primary reason for not having a car, then you've just sentenced yourself to guaranteed failure, or at the very least, a lifetime of low-level nagging guilt. Some friend will offer you a ride on a rainy day and instead of feeling grateful, you'll feel bad for accepting it. (That friend, by the way, will think you're a hypocritical moron.) You'll feel bad for flying in a plane to visit your ailing grandmother, and you might even feel bad for breathing. Even if that's morally consistent, it's no way to live in a modern first world country, and it's also not going to help the environment in any significant way. If you're actually able to pull off a major lifestyle change based on concerns over carbon emissions, you won't have too many followers, and you might even turn people off so much that you hurt the cause.

Luckily for my own psychological health, I don't do this carless thing for the "right" reasons. I do it for three practical, conservative reasons. One: I am lazy, and if I had a car, I probably wouldn't ride my bike much, which would be bad since I'm also a glutton and that bike is about the only thing standing between me and the number "300" on the scale. Two: When I am more-or-less forced to ride my bike to do normal everyday things like commuting to work, I find the exercise makes me feel better and so I enjoy life more. Three: I am a huge cheapskate and cars are expensive.

Wasn't that easy? Remove the morality play, and the whole business ceases to be a bit of cultish signaling meant to identify me with the sanctified "in" group. It doesn't mean I don't care about the environment, possibly for deeply moral reasons. It's just not necessary to talk about it that way.

Framing the question without the morality also takes away the equal and opposite reaction of the "out" group that I would have been implicitly criticizing as immoral. No doubt they would have instantly identified the slight, felt threatened, turned up the defense, and come up with all kinds of reasons why not owning a car for environmental reasons is stupid. The bicycle-related identity politics battle lines thusly drawn, they would go out of their way to own bigger cars and never ride bikes. And it's possible that riding a bike itself would soon be seen as mildly traitorous – a sign that you're with the granolas – further discouraging anyone in the "out" group from taking up such a refreshing hobby in the first place. Before you can say "350 parts per million," a carbon dioxide problem that could wreak havoc on many generations to come turns into a battle of dueling lifestyle accessories. As it already has.

But how can anyone argue against "getting exercise makes me feel good" or "cars are expensive?" Really, they would never even need to go there, since nobody got threatened with immoral "out" group status in the first place. "There goes Peter again," they would say, "trying not to weigh 300 pounds. Good luck and Godspeed and I wonder what's on TV."

Being liberal for the "right" reasons instantly creates identity politics on both sides. But being liberal for practical, reasonable, conservative reasons disarms people and makes your own life easier, since you don't have to think about your sins all the time. And maybe, just maybe, it also makes some space for the good people of Pennsylvania, Wisconsin, and Michigan to notice that they agree with your policy agenda – the one formerly obscured by the smug.

Growing up on the left side of the spectrum, I swam in the glorious stories of people who defiantly sat at segregated lunch counters, built trails for the Civilian Conservation Corps, invented public radio, and created the concept of the weekend. We relished those wins, because liberals are all about making life better and richer for everybody. We're supposed to take Hobbes' comments about life being "nasty, brutish, and short" as a challenge.

But what have we done for America lately? Obamacare? Dodd-

Frank? Perhaps gay marriage? Ruth Bader Ginsburg? It's not nothing, but how are we doing on childcare, the environment, healthcare access, gun safety, living wages, affordable college, and universal preschool? Given that the people are with us on all those issues, shouldn't our post-Great-Society resume be a bit longer?

It could be. It should be. But we have to win elections first. We have to quit isolating ourselves in our own moral righteousness. We have to be liberal, but for conservative reasons.

PETER RICE

Chapter Two

_____

Poverty, welfare, a dead Greek dude, and 1,900 years of complaining.

SO THERE YOU GO with your fully loaded and tricked out modern society: You took the trouble to build schools, roads, houses, factories, a reliable power grid, and refrigerators. You procured natural resources, created jobs in accounts receivable, *and invented beer*. All in all, nice work! We really like what you've done here.

But just as you're about to call it a day and kick back with one of those beers from one of those refrigerators, you notice a bug in this otherwise flawless system. Some people, for God knows what reason, simply can't figure out how to work it, and they're just sort of flopping around all hopeless like. *But it's so simple*, you think. Just get one of these jobs, exchange your labor for the local currency, then convert that into food and shelter and AC/DC tribute band tickets and whatever else you may need. So you screw up your courage, and actually say all that out loud. But it's a total flop.

These people – poor people – just continue to fail at life, and your puzzlement soon turns to anger. What the hell is their problem, you think. Everything they need is there. Is it really as hard as they make it look? So you compare notes with some friends and discover that they've had similar thoughts.

All that, of course, creates a vacuum that professional commentators rush to fill.

"There's nothing wrong with poverty in itself," they say. "We just have a problem with lazy people who drink too much and make stupid decisions to further mess up their wretched lives."

You can probably think of various pundits who have said things like this. You can probably imagine Paul Ryan saying it over one of those beers back home in Wisconsin. Maybe you yourself have said it. You're certainly in good company, because that's actually a quote from Plutarch, the philosopher/writer who died nearly 1,900 years ago, translated to modern informality.

Since his day, we've figured out the roundness of the Earth, worked out that it actually orbits the sun, and invented several helpful WhatsApp emojis, but the debate on what to do with all those poor people has barely budged an inch. We're still fine with poor people in theory, and so long as they are sober, industrious, righteous, and brave (Plutarch's actual words), we're happy to help with whatever they need. But this wildly unattractive sort that abuses substances, commits crimes, reproduces too much, and does other moronic and disagreeable things that contribute to the poverty – it's them we dislike so intensely and wish to avoid helping at all costs.

In the United States, we responded to this predictably enough, mainly by helping the poor people we like. Specifically, old people, who have a pretty decent excuse for not getting one of those jobs, all things considered. We write them checks every so often (Social Security) and pay doctors to take care of them (Medicare). Combined, that represents roughly half of all federal spending, which is pretty impressive for a country that doesn't think of itself as a socialist welfare state. All in all, it really helps to reduce poverty for lots of sober and industrious people who, previously, were in a pretty bad fix when they got too old to work and the medical bills started piling up.

Later, we also started the Children's Health Insurance Program, because we like kids, even if their parents might happen to be poor people we don't like. And then there's the Earned Income Tax Credit, which transfers all kinds of money to poor people who have earned income, a pretty good indication of industriousness if ever there was one. Long story short: By the turn of the century, we were doing a pretty bang up job helping the good poor people.

While we were at it, we also created a few dramatically smaller initiatives to help the poor people we didn't like, if only incidentally. There was unemployment insurance, which was kind of a mixed bag, since it essentially paid people not to work. The poor people we liked definitely benefited and used it sparingly, but we sure did notice when the poor people we didn't like used it, often for longer than we would've preferred. Disability insurance worked like that as well: There was a clear need for it, but some people's need was clearer than others. Same with Medicaid, food stamps, and in some rare cases that nonetheless get tons of press, direct cash assistance to poor families.

The lefties who enacted these programs always sold them by talking about how they would help deserving poor people we liked, and this might have actually worked if all of the people who got the benefits lived in a hermetically-sealed compound in rural Nevada. Or perhaps just never mentioned it. But word got out pretty quick that some people at the grocery store using *that card* were not actually having to pay for their food, which all-too-often was much nicer than the food the rest of us were rolling down the conveyor belt at checkout. Others compared medical bills and noticed some pretty striking differences in the "amount due" area. Still others couldn't help but notice that while "disabled" neighbors apparently qualified under some government definition of the term, it did not match the picture in their heads. Nor did the daily routines of still other neighbors match the popular conception of a "rigorous job search."

This provoked a smoldering rage for a while, until people noticed something else: Some of the recipients of government help were jerks or just generally did not have their act together. They were easy to spot, of course, since jerks tend to stand out. And at that point, the smoldering rage turned into blind fury. Our best laid plans to avoid helping the bad poor people had been foiled while we weren't looking.

Conservatives really hated this state of affairs, and took to ranting about it constantly. Of course, they were egged on by A.M. talk radio, and for some, there was probably a racial or other "otherizing" element or two in play. But at the core, this hatred of helping people who they reckoned could stand to kick it up a notch in life was just a combination of normal human responses and personal experience.

Think of it this way: For most of human history, until very recently, humans lived in small tribal settings where everyone depended on everyone else to pull their weight, because every day was a struggle to get enough calories to survive. You can still see some of this in poorer countries, where children are more likely to help out with the housework or the family business and less likely to have a protracted adolescence involving lots of leisure time. Old people, meanwhile, don't exactly retire as much as they spend more time helping with the grandkids, or perhaps starting some light side project that brings in a trickle of income, because every little bit helps.

But in first world countries at least, we are so rich that we can actually afford to have large groups of people doing nothing productive whatsoever. Children often have only token chores to perform around the house, and many never really contribute anything significant to the family's financial position. After college, reams of 20-somethings with well-heeled parents routinely spend years finding themselves and not doing much of anything. And while plenty of retirees volunteer, help with grandkids, or just plain work normal jobs, plenty more check out of the productive flow, buy an RV, and galavant around the country making the most of the screaming good deal that is the senior national parks pass.

And then, of course, there are the people we don't like: working age, able-bodied, but not working. Or maybe they do work, but had too many kids before they got their life's financial house in order, so we suddenly have to help out. Or maybe they turned dubious lower back pain into a regular disability check. Or they dropped out of middle school to pursue a life of drug use and petty burglary. Could be a lot of scenarios. But whatever the case, we end up transferring wealth to these people and their mistakes.

For most of human history, such a state of affairs was impossible, because mass idleness would threaten the pursuit of calories and thus the survival of the group. So it's no surprise that many people, most vocally conservatives, are mad as hell about it. Getting angry about other people not being productive or otherwise dragging down the group is a perfectly natural human reaction, especially when they are using your money to do it. (You may recall having a boss who felt this way.)

The liberal response to this perfectly normal, natural, and logical vitriol is to throw budget figures and empathy at the problem. We can afford it, they say, correctly pointing out that the controversial outlays that attract all the ire are little more than a rounding error in the federal budget. Why not go take a look at defense appropriations, they ask, and see if you can't throw a tantrum about some of that money? (Of course this does not play well, since conservatives are, if only at a subliminal level, worried about the survival of our society, and not terribly interested in gutting the part of the government designed to guarantee it.)

Liberals proceed to a strangely bifurcated discussion, first arguing that the people on welfare are by and large not jerks, but rather good folks just temporarily down on their luck. And even if there are some jerks in the system, they continue, they are basically doing the best they can with the terrible hand that life dealt them. Have you ever walked a mile in the tattered shoes of a homeless person? Do you know how hard it is to find childcare when you're poor? How can you sit there with your comfortable life while people go without? Here, let me tell you a sad story about a single mom who had a horrible childhood and now has five kids...

Liberals come out of the argument looking like patronizing wimps with nothing to offer but loser talk. They bring up the small budget figures, of course, but the size of the line item isn't actually the problem. The problem is a deeply felt, instinctual perception that it's a total waste of money and hurting the larger group. Talking about the numbers like that is a bit like telling someone who is afraid of flying about how they're more likely to die on the way to the airport: It seems like it should work, but it never does. Meanwhile, liberals appear to be arguing for this spending on the grounds that's it's merely a small waste of money, which is probably not helping the cause much.

Sob stories about hard luck cases don't do any better. Liberals hear about the single mom with five kids, or the 40ish disabled addict, and think to themselves, "sounds awful – let me open my wallet and ease the pain." Most others hear those stories and think, "I worked for this money and would really like to keep it if that's okay." Or, "how did this horrible childhood of hers somehow never include the opportunity to access birth control?" Or, "how is it that I have managed to deal with my own problems without becoming a long-term public charge?"

Statements like this are deemed by liberals to be heartless and mean and sometimes racist, like, presumably, the conservatives who uttered them. And predictably, accusing the opposition of not caring about people turns out to be a less-than-effective way to make political friends, not least because it is so, so, not even close to being true.

Conservatives, you see, give more money to charity than liberals, even factoring out contributions to religious organizations. Or maybe we shouldn't factor that out, since churches are often out on the front lines, rendering social services to the needy, especially refugees and the victims of sex trafficking. Turns out those heartless bastards have been in the helping business for a long time.

Conservatives also increasingly live in poorer rural areas full of people *who are actually on welfare.* The ten states with the most people of working age on disability are Michigan, Missouri, South Carolina, Tennessee, Maine, Mississippi, Kentucky, Alabama, Arkansas, and West Virginia (2011 numbers). Only Maine voted for Clinton, and then by only three points. It's safe to say that residents of these highly Republican states could tell you plenty of stories that are probably even more heart-wrenching than the anecdotes filtering up to the urban hipsterdoms full of rich Democrats. They could also recite chapter and verse the contextual problems with schools, broken families, the economy, morons in local government, addiction, childhood trauma, and every other depressing ingredient in the poverty soup.

They live in it, but they don't like it. Like any other proud American, it probably kills them to think about their home turf like that. They might sooner vote for someone who acknowledges the reality they live in and how pissed off they are about it over someone who brushes it aside with pedantic arguments and appeals to empathy that don't address the core poverty problem.

That's the real shame of the liberal rhetorical strategy: We've managed to take a bunch of people who, by and large, love people and are pretty keen to help, and driven them into the hands of the party of Wall Street because they didn't share the same narrative about the problem or emote the correct responses to the right parts of it. To borrow from Wendell Berry, we took a majority solution and neatly divided it into two problems.

Being a liberal has never been easy. We're the side, as Robert F. Kennedy put it, that "dream[s] of things that never were, and ask[s], why not," which is hard work. They are the side that, as William F. Buckley put it, "stands athwart history yelling 'Stop!'" Which is about as easy as politics gets. Such is our lot as the side that is always advocating for change and for the weakest members of society.

But how many elections must we lose because we look like naive and indulgent chumps, all too happy to tax people who work hard only to give the proceeds to those who don't, while telling everyone they should be happy about it because there but for the grace of God go you? Why couldn't we prosecute the war on poverty in a way that does more than just keep people alive and treading water? What's a liberal for conservative reasons to do here?

A good start would be to stop papering over the reality: Lots of thoroughly disagreeable people are on welfare, and we don't have to like them or empathize with them. While many or even most just use the system for a little while, too many people are on it for too long, and those who gamed their way in deserve to be kicked the hell off. Too many people are not working, even though they could, and that's an economic and personal tragedy.

Now that we have the attention of conservatives, earned by acknowledging realities liberals aren't supposed to talk about, we press the attack on the right-wing non agenda: If they had their way, the conservatives would just end these programs. Just what we need: Millions of poor desperate people who suddenly have trouble eating, getting vaccines, and sheltering themselves. What could possibly go wrong?

In the conservative imagination, all these out-of-work coal miners in West Virginia and opioid addicts in northern New Mexico would wake up the next morning with fresh motivation, go get MBAs, and be working for Goldman Sachs by the end of next week. They imagine that welfare is the thing actually creating the poverty, which I suppose implies that it didn't exist before F.D.R. callously invented the modern welfare state.

Back in reality, we know that yanking all the money won't work. Sure, it might jolt a few people out of their complacency and into a higher income bracket, but not most people. Throughout history, the poor have always been with us, whether there was a government available to help or not. Having a bunch of people lying in doorways all night, hanging around the streets, and festering in moldy trailers down dirt roads has never served our interests. Not today, and not when they put that line about the poor always being with us into the Gospel of Matthew (26:11). The neglect just breeds crime and disease, diminishes property values, and makes it that much harder for the next generation to break out into something better.

Conservative non-alternative vanquished, sell the agenda: Welfare may keep people fed and off the streets, and on the whole that's a good thing, but it doesn't solve the core problem. So here's the liberal agenda on welfare and poverty: Nobody starves, nobody suffers from preventable medical problems, everybody who possibly can works, *and we actually try to solve the problem.*

How do we get there? That's another, much longer book, but here's a quick taste of the innovative reforms we can promote if we can move the debate beyond whether we like poor people or not:

- Do more to help people move from depressed areas to boom areas.
- Universal preschool, so all kids get the kind of social software they're sure to need in the modern, collaborative workforce.
- Zero out all those fees that make it tough for low-income kids to play school sports, the better to make sure they're off the streets and around positive role models teaching good life skills.
- Home visitation for all newborn babies by a registered nurse or other qualified professional, to identify and address mental and physical health hazards before they impact the child.

- Wage insurance, which incentivises finding new work as soon as possible after a layoff by throwing in a few extra dollars per hour if the new gig doesn't pay as well as the old.
- Make sure every at-risk kid has a Big Brother/Big Sister-type mentor.

We could go on. There are lots of things we could do as a society to fight poverty that are intuitively popular, easy to talk about, not politically polarizing, and not very expensive. But we'll never get a chance to make that case if we spend all our time fighting about cash and in kind services and defending the sometimes disagreeable people who use them.

That's why we should help the poor by doing more than talking about the plight of poor people all day. We need to point out something conservatives can't argue with: When people, for whatever reason, can't figure modern society out, problems crop up and they get dumped in the laps of those of us who can. Complaining about that hasn't worked for at least 1,900 years, and making it harder to eat isn't going to help either. It's time to actually solve the problem.

We need to position ourselves as the side that sees the grim, unromanticized reality of welfare and poverty on the ground, and has some promising ideas for making it better. That's the sort of agenda that could make us a few friends who could, in turn, help us make a few laws.

PETER RICE

Chapter Three

_____

To read this chapter in English, press one.

Capitulo Tres

_____

Para leer en español, marque dos.

THIS ALL STARTED INNOCENTLY ENOUGH.

Back in the mid-1800s, we couldn't help but notice that our good neighbor, Mexico, really seemed to be loaded down with a lot of excess territory. So we did what any good hiking buddy will do for a friend and generously relieved them of about one third of the heavy burden, including Texas, New Mexico, Arizona, and California.

They somehow forgot to thank us for this kind gesture, known there as the *Intervención estadounidense en México*. Perhaps the card got lost in the mail. But no matter. The upshot is that the United States, and the proud ranks of American citizens, suddenly included not a few Spanish-speaking Mexicans who lived in Spanish-named towns.

For quite a long time, *those people* generally (and considerately) confined themselves to that homebase of southwestern states. And given the history, it was kind of hard to get all riled up about it. Plus there weren't that many of them anyway. But between 1980 and 2014, reports the Pew Hispanic Center, the Hispanic population grew to around 55 million, up from 14 million, with a strong flow of foreign-born immigrants bolstering an expanding native-born population.

People came from all parts of Mexico. Some Mexicans even came from Costa Rica, Guatemala, Honduras, the Dominican Republic, Colombia, and Peru, and claimed to know nothing about this tequila and mariachi business. Still other Mexicans, hilariously claiming to be American citizens, came from Puerto Rico. And once in awhile you would even run into a Mexican in Santa Fe or Taos who was more than happy to inform you that their family had been living in the United States since before it was the United States. Just the sort of goofy antics we've come to expect from the Mexicans.

Apparently not content to spend all their time in California, Arizona, and New Mexico, they started showing up in places like North Dakota, Minnesota, Virginia, Georgia, and Iowa. As if their mere presence wasn't jarring enough, many of them took the bold step of communicating amongst themselves in their native language. (You know, *Mexican*.) Of course they should have known better, but they callously ploughed on, opening businesses, sending their kids to school, and worst of all, obtaining gainful employment.

This caused, borrowing a term never to my knowledge used by the

Pew Hispanic Center, a total four-alarm freakout. Conservatives, being the "stay the same" people, led the meltdown, pointing out that immigration was "out of control," that immigrants were gobbling up government services, and that, horror of horrors, honest white Americans were forced to press "one" for English on automated phone systems. (This alone seems to animate about 50 percent of anti-immigrant sentiment, for reasons that escape me entirely. But by all means, get back to us if you end up having to press "two" for English.)

Not helping public relations matters was the fact that many immigrants had entered the country illegally (or, often, entered legally and stayed past a key deadline). Conservatives, as the law and order types, really didn't like that. Pretty soon, the mantra of building the wall started, as if the country whose ingenious citizens invented the birth control pill, the color TV, the Caesar Salad, and the Salma Hayek would be totally stumped by ladders.

To counter this foolishness, liberals predictably deployed the most annoying arguments they could come up with. Immigrants are wonderful, hard-working people, they assured the freakout cases. They just want to do jobs that nobody else wants to do and support their families. Besides, they said, as sanctimony alarms rang out all over the land, we are a nation of immigrants – a diverse and vibrant rainbow patchwork of cultures, languages, and religions, but together we are one people, one human family, and we can coexist in harmony.

This went over like a lead balloon, since the component parts are easy to disprove, completely irrelevant, and do nothing to check the fear driving the conservatives. In fact they seem to hint at even more immigration and the breakdown of national borders.

Arguing that immigrants are basically good people may be supported by the stats that show they're less likely than native-born Americans to commit crimes, and it sure resonates with those of us who know a few of them. But it's a bit of a stretch to imply/promise that a group numbering in the tens of millions won't include a few ne'er-do-well bullies and criminals. Still, the liberals cling to it anyway, and every time an immigrant ends up in trouble with the law, for anything from littering to first degree murder, the illusion bubble is popped. Those conservatives who can't vouch for a few immigrants personally have nothing to hang their hat on but the promise that there will be more and more of this "we are the world" parade coming soon to a small, predominantly white town near you.

Conservatives didn't realize that the melting pot meant we could no longer have an immigration policy. Sure, they thought, we're a nation of immigrants, but there's no law saying we *have* to be a nation of *those* immigrants. And so the freakout continued, supplemented somewhere along the line with the bit about "stealing our jobs."

Liberals and their immigrant allies eventually upped the ante by gaining a bit of political power and using it to create the atrociously named "sanctuary" cities. They also came up with the term "undocumented" to replace "illegal," on the theory that no human being is "illegal" and that it would be handy to have a easy linguistic marker distinguishing the good hip people who are down with immigrants from the bad racists who are not.

This just made conservatives angrier, because the opposition was plainly and proudly ignoring the law or not enforcing it, albeit in a sort of passive aggressive way, and because "undocumented" is two syllables longer than "illegal." The term also seems to imply that the people in question didn't actually break the law, but rather had the proper paperwork then forgot where they put it.

And so once again, liberals carry the cross of human dignity to the most harrowing place on the map of political loser talk, defending people who broke laws, implying that borders shouldn't really be a thing, and pleading for the acceptance of all people, all the while hoping against hope that no immigrant will ever get in trouble with the law. And, probably because it seems crass, they rarely mention immigration's very real upsides.

Luckily, liberals for conservative reasons are not afraid of crass. So the argument in favor of immigration from Latin America jettisons the unconditional love and the "coexist" bumper stickers in favor of capitalism, cash, and ballsy offense plays.

So these people are swarming unchecked into the country? Like hell they are. *We invited them.* American businesses are happy to hire them, and we are happy to eat the food they harvest, live in the houses they build and clean, and wasn't Diego Luna just terrific in the last Star Wars movie? Yes, he was (and to the best of our knowledge, quite documented).

This is about capitalism and free markets, and if a business here wants to enter into a voluntary employment contract with a foreign national, it is their right and none of your concern. People do not risk their lives crossing the Arizona desert because they enjoy wilderness backpacking. They want a job, we want to give them one, and the legal options for making that happen range from convoluted to impossible.

We liberals like to call that big government getting in the way of entrepreneurs trying to create jobs, and it needs to stop. We need a system where anyone with an employment offer can come on over and do what they do best without a lot of mindless regulatory interference. Because the last thing we need to do is disrupt the supply or increase the cost of food and shelter. Also, a lot of old white people here are looking to me for their Social Security checks, and I would appreciate some backup.

So let's end this foolish chatter about "illegal immigrants," and quit beating around the bush with weak-sauce arguments about poor people just trying to feed their poor families. Let's just come out and say this: Whatever law made these people illegal is about the dumbest jumble of word vomit ever to hit parchment paper. The pathetic collection of scatterbrained halfwits that wrote it were clearly trying to choke off the normal willing-buyer-willing-seller relationships of the marketplace. It's hurting *our* businesses and *our* access to goods and services for no good reason and that line of commie horse clop doesn't have any place in the land of the free.

American business has, despite this big government yolk, managed to assemble all kinds of talent from all over the world, which makes us rich and ensures that we can have the best of everything. That goes for every sector of the economy, from construction to agriculture to tech and medicine. If we can attract lots of people who are smart or hard-working or resourceful or all of the above, the brilliance that emerges will create jobs and reinforce American cultural and economic dominance in the world.

Besides, we all want to make sure that the problems of Latin America do not become our problems, and letting immigrants in is a great way to do that. That's because while they've actually made great strides in recent decades in the stable government department (nobody worries much about Chile and Argentina anymore), there's still a lot of poverty, and corruption that entrenches it. Our neighbors to the south are quite simply not as economically stable as our neighbor to the north, and there's always a danger that problems down there could show up here. (As a general rule, you don't want to ignore problems "down there.")

One way to keep things stable is foreign aid, but that's a huge drag because it involves taxation and inefficient governments or nonprofits that at best are only guessing about what will actually improve things. A better way is to allow immigration, because lots of those workers send impressive portions of their paychecks back home to rural hamlets often lacking decent plumbing or luxuries like floors. So we end up doing the most efficient form of foreign aid imaginable, since it's free for us and administered by NGOs called "families" who know exactly what is required back home. And we even get useful labor out of the deal.

Right now in rural Guatemala there's probably some guy totally pissed off at his spectacularly hopeless government and he's just about ready to join some machete-wielding friends in the plaza to demand its ouster. But instead, he spends the day at home supervising the installation of a tile floor (to replace the dirt), the placement of a new table on that floor, and the eating of real food on that table, all thanks to some cousin washing dishes at a Denny's near Allentown, Pennsylvania. After all that, he's very content and totally pooped, so he thinks to himself: "well, guess I'll overthrow the government some other day."

Who knows how exactly, but that machete-wielding mob probably would have turned into our problem eventually. Maybe it would've caused a flood of refugees without immediate job connections to wash up on American shores. Maybe it would put some critical trade route in jeopardy and we'd have to send the Marines down to regulate. Maybe it would just cause problems for other neighboring countries and distract from some other project we were trying to do with them. But instead of dealing with the fallout, we can just let some poor devil wash dishes, which seems much easier.

With all that extra free time, we can tackle these so-called "sanctuary cities," a collection of municipalities (and counties and states) that don't allow their various and sundry law enforcement units to cooperate with federal immigration authorities. Basically, it's a great idea with a terrible name, and these places end up coming off as smug liberal enclaves flipping off law-and-order types with a loaded word that evokes righteous protection for people who have broken laws.

Which is a shame, because as much as it's tempting to flip off law-and-order types these days, that's not at all why I, a homeowner in the sanctuary city known as Albuquerque, want to keep things as they are. I'm just looking out for number one.

The 87102 zip code includes the city zoo, a number of excellent restaurants and coffee shops, the Amtrak station, fun microbreweries, and my house. About 20,000 people live there, according to the Census, and 47 percent of them have some kind of Mexican origin. How many of them are illegal (sorry, *undocumented*) immigrants? Hard to say for sure, but the Census, which doesn't care about legal status when it sends out the counters, says there are 3,500 foreign born people in the zip code. No doubt most of them are perfectly legal, but it wouldn't surprise me one bit to learn that 1,000 people living a short walk from my house are not technically supposed to be in the country. And since "mixed status" households are about as common in Albuquerque as sunny days, those people could easily be spread over a much larger number of families. I'm well aware that this group and the larger neighborhood includes a not-insignificant number of scumbags, but on the whole it's a great bunch of folks who can be counted on to keep up their places, say "hi" over the fence, and most critically of all, call the cops if they see something amiss.

This is why local law enforcement should never deputize themselves as immigration agents: Because we have a term for neighborhoods in America where residents don't trust the cops – bad neighborhoods. How they got here, whether they've got the right paperwork, and their fundamental humanity doesn't matter a bit. What matters is that they're here, and if they see something, they need to feel perfectly comfortable saying something, because it's my property and my life on the line. They had better be able to call 911, get interviewed by cops, and testify in court, all in Spanish if that's what they need. Hell, they should be able to do it in Ancient Greek or Esperanto – whatever makes 'em happy. Above all, they should be able to do it without fear that they or the old man or grandma will get shipped back to Chihuahua, all because they decided to give a damn about my stuff and my personal safety.

There's another reason: Cooperating with federal immigration authorities takes time, and the cops should be spending that time going after real crime and real criminals. We have plenty of both in Albuquerque, and if some of it happens to come together in the form of an incident in front of my house, the cops had better not delay their response because they were arranging for some roofer to get deported. The feds are more than welcome to play their silly cat-and-mouse game along the border, but just speaking here as a white native-born homeowner concerned about property values, I would appreciate them leaving my local cops the hell out of it. The sanctuary is for me.

Still, we need to rebrand this sensible local solution right away. Maybe we're not a sanctuary city anymore, but a city that leaves

Federal Laws to the Feds (A FLF city!). Or call it a city that renders unto Caesar what is Caesar's, or whatever. Obviously, I shouldn't be in charge of this.

The situation is different, but not radically different, in Dubuque, Iowa and Jackson, Mississippi and every other hamlet, village, and farm in our country. There are people wandering around everywhere who are technically supposed to be wandering around in a different country, but even if we wanted to abandon our capitalist principles and kick them out, it's cost prohibitive, logistically near-impossible, and not something that's going to happen anytime soon.

Which is yet another reason we need an immigration system that takes into account the realities of business. The chile patch in Hatch, New Mexico and the startup in San Francisco could really use some immigrant help, and they need a easy and sensible system they can navigate to make it happen. But so long as the screaming match continues, with its cries of broken laws and pressing one for English on one hand, and conversation-stopping accusations of racism on the other, we will probably never get there.

And that's the true shame. Because we fight about immigration like it's about the immigrants, when really it's about all of us. Our wealth, our free-market economy, and our neighborhoods are at stake. We liberals can cross our fingers and hope that demographic realities give us a majority on this issue one day. But if we shifted focus from heart-wrenching narratives, talked about real concerns that larger groups of Americans can identify with, and generally grew a pair, we might be able to win today.

PETER RICE

Chapter Four

Islam, refugees, and underwhelming home improvement projects.

MOST IMMIGRATION IN THE UNITED STATES is a fairly boring and orderly trickle of a process. Somebody's wizened old uncle comes over to join the family so they can take care of him. Or maybe a company arranges for a worker's passage. Or some American travels abroad, falls in love, and brings back someone to live happily ever after with. I can already hear you snoring.

Even the allegedly out-of-control illegal immigration from Latin America is actually quite orderly, since basically everyone down there (seriously, everyone – it's amazing) has family or friends up here that stand ready to help with cultural adjustment and employment connections. As anyone who has ever traveled anywhere can tell you, these little things go a long way.

Refugees, on the other hand, have a tougher time of it. There they were, minding their own business and more-or-less content to keep at it, when some war, famine, credible death threat, or other catastrophe forced their hand and here they are.

Normally, people have a chance to psych themselves up before getting on the boat. They can do research, learn a few phrases of the new language, line up connections, and take care of the little things like *packing a bag*. They can also self-select: Not everyone is cut out for the stress of leaving the home country, after all. Refugees often do not have this luxury, and for less populous groups, there's not necessarily a mini-version of your hometown somewhere in the United States where you can catch up on the gossip from the old country and eat at a restaurant that makes that one dish just like your mom did.

We've taken in a few million refugees since the fall of Saigon in 1975. Besides Vietnam, they came from the former Soviet Union, the former Yugoslavia, Iraq, Myanmar, and other places that did not at the time count as ideal vacation spots. Many years on, these admissions do not stand out as revolutionary acts that swayed presidential elections.

Not so for the poor souls in Syria. There are about 5 million refugees from that civil war (more counting internally displaced people), and while most have stuck close to the neighborhood, in places like Turkey and Lebanon, just under one million have applied for asylum in Europe (says the UN), as of this writing. A little over 10,000 made it to the U.S. before President "I Think I'm a Nice Person" issued the now famous ban.

Liberals, of course, are in favor of refugee resettlement in the United States and the more the merrier. That's because we love other cultures, and as residents of big diverse cities, we're pretty invested in the whole melting pot idea. We especially like to help out people fleeing war-torn countries, because it doesn't get more bleeding-heart than meeting some tired poor huddled masses at the airport and taking them home.

Conservatives, with some notable faith-based exceptions, are more instinctively opposed to this idea. They're generally the "stay-the-same" side and nothing says "change" quite like inviting a bunch of strangers over. They're also quite riled up about Islam and many of its trappings, especially the various categories of headscarf that nobody can ever keep straight. They will quickly insinuate that some of these refugees could well be terrorists, coming as they do from a bad neighborhood partially controlled by the Islamic State. They've been freaked out by this for quite a while, in fact, and it often manifests as fights over the construction of mosques and the apparently genuine fear that Sharia law will one day reign supreme over Oklahoma.

Liberals respond to this with a predictably annoying and not comforting set of statistics and deflections. Islam is one of the world's great religions, they say, firmly lodged in the Abrahamic tradition with Christianity and Judaism. Crazy overwhelming majorities of Muslims are not terrorists, they continue, and you're more likely to die from the slow accumulation of swallowed chewing gum than in an attack. And no refugee, from Syria or anywhere else, has killed an American in a terrorist attack since we set up the modern system in 1980. Terrorism is more likely to be the work of native born Americans (San Bernardino, Orlando) than refugees. Besides, they add, a lot of these refugees are actually Christians! C'mon, y'all love Christians!

For some reason, we keep thinking this line of argument will work. Of course Islam is a big deal on the world religion front, but since when has a common ancestor spelled peace? The Catholics and Protestants in Northern Ireland had a common ancestor. Same with the Sunni and Shia in Iraq. And *of course* most Muslims are not terrorists, *but most terrorists we see on TV are Muslims*. Also thanks for pointing out that we may not have to worry about these people, but we definitely have to worry about their American-born kids – really makes us feel better. Why must we solve all of the world's problems like this anyway? Why is this our risk to take? And the Christians look exactly like the Muslims, so that doesn't help much, but we do notice how often you defend Muslims by talking about Christians, and we think it's curious. It's as though you liberals are also afraid of the terrorism danger but too politically correct to admit it. It's as though you read about every new mass shooting or bombing with your fingers crossed, hoping it's merely some loner white guy who grew up Presbyterian.

Sensing islamophobia, liberals will at this point shift from arguing that Muslims are great folks to arguing that terrorist attacks don't have anything to do with Islam. Once again, it's a fair academic point: Just because some young man *said* he killed a bunch of people for Islamic reasons, it does not automatically follow that we should *believe* him. These guys are spinning us and they're spinning themselves, just like when the White House budget director says cutting Meals on Wheels is an act of kindness.

Islam, the liberal argument goes, is just a convenient cover story. Nobody is going to justify murder by saying they were just a disconnected and angry loner who latched onto a violent ideology because it made them feel important and powerful. Certainly not when a poorly-understood major religion is available for sublet, in any event. From that point of view, there's no significant difference between Charleston church shooter Dylann Roof and Orlando nightclub shooter Omar Mateen. It's about social isolation and angry young men, not Islam.

The argument makes a few reasonable points, but falls flat anyway. To begin with, we're not terribly good at deciphering spin, especially when it concerns a subject like Islam that people don't know anything about. If someone said a terrorist act was about Christianity, we'd just make a quick mental list of the dozens of Christians we personally know that would never do such a thing and then conclude that that bad guy was full of it. But there aren't enough Muslims in America for most of us to make that list, so if some deranged psychopath says it's about Islam, we give him the benefit of the doubt, and that's probably not going to change.

But even if there is not a causal relationship between Islam and terrorism, a correlation is enough to give conservatives pause when reflecting on the possibility of admitting more Muslim refugees, to say nothing of the suspicion they hold for the Muslims who are already here.

Most of all, the liberal argument falls flat because academic posturing is not going to change how humans are wired. We're all afraid of death, of course, but we are especially afraid when it involves dramatic, strange, or random circumstances, even if the odds are astronomically against them ever coming to pass. If we were really concerned about what was going to do us in, we'd stop eating white bread and sugar and join gyms. We would spend a lot of time fretting about obesity, preventable medical errors, smoking, and drinking too much. But instead we worry about terrorism, not being able to see a woman's face, shark attacks, airplane crashes, and in a former bygone era, quicksand.

So quite naturally, conservatives are having none of it. They value security highly, and are not impressed by arguments about odds because they don't care about the melting pot diversity dream so there's no upside either way. So they argue that the cultures are not compatible, point to some kid somewhere who didn't show proper respect to a female teacher for cultural reasons, wax on about how we don't want them to "take over," and by then we're off the races.

Speaking of races, liberals at this point end the argument by calling the conservatives racist, all while trying to spin the cultural adjustment piece as a seamless weekend getaway of a process rather than a multi-generational slog full of identity crises and occasional clashes with the traditions of the new country.

So in the end, liberals for liberal reasons try to sell conservatives using liberal values, give them nothing of what they want, promise more of what they don't want, call them racists for not biting, and generally come off as stupid or naive to everyone who is not already on board. Liberals for conservative reasons, of course, will take a very different approach: On American Muslims in general, replace weak defense with strong offense. And on American refugee policy, focus on solving the damn problem.

The problem, in the liberal imagination, seems to be the exact number of Syrians getting off airplanes in the United States and receiving emotional greetings from do-gooder Americans. Obama made that happen for 10,000 people, and Hillary Clinton talked about bumping it up to 65,000. But that represents .2 and 1.3 percent of the total refugee population, respectively. Not nothing, but not exactly game-changing problem solving either. Liberals are trying to address a small slice of the problem in a tangible, emotional, highly visible, and self-gratifying way that actually does very little. Which comes naturally to us: Recycling and hybrid cars fall into the same category.

The real problem is that about five million people are hanging around, completely disconnected from normal life, often with limited local language abilities, skill sets ranging from medical degree to town drunk, with no place to go. And they're doing it in a neighborhood teeming with Americans and American interests.

By way of review, let's take a quick tour: Syria borders Turkey, Iraq, Jordan, Israel, and Lebanon, and is quite close to Cypress. We have military personnel stationed right now in Turkey, Cyprus, and Iraq, and a long-standing commitment to be thoroughly involved in Israel's security. Jordan is a friend and one of the few Arab countries to have made peace with Israel. We're also quite fond of consuming petroleum products from the region. And most of the refugees that fled the region went to European NATO allies who are major trading and diplomacy partners.

You may think this level of involvement is terrible foreign policy, but that doesn't make it less real. Millions of displaced people wandering around or boxed up in crowded camps in a region with American interests too numerous to count means that we had better solve this problem before it creates several new and bigger ones.

We've already seen what can happen when a small fraction of the group gets a wild hair and decides to emigrate over to Europe. What else might a group of a few million desperate people without much to lose be capable of? The answer is simple: We don't want to find out. We've dealt with instability in the Middle East before, and if usually involves ungodly amounts of money and many new rows of white headstones at national cemeteries. So let's not go there.

But if millions of people getting uprooted halfway around the world means we should do what we need to do to solve the problem and prevent future problems, it does not necessarily mean everyone should pack their bags and move to America. Lots of refugees end up returning home, which is probably a good thing for the rebuilding that will have to happen eventually. And there may be some real advantages to keeping them close by, especially in Arabic-speaking countries. The exact strategy is best left to actual experts in other books, but at a minimum, we should be ready to help our allies in the Middle East and Europe with logistics and cash. (We have done some of this, but who knows where the new administration will take it.) That said, it may well be that the best strategy is to continue settling some small fraction of them in the West, and if that's the plan, we should probably take a few if only to show the Europeans we're team players.

Could some of them be terrorists? Not likely, but sure, it's possible. Will a few of them have such hopelessly backward opinions on the role of women in society that conservatives long for the comforting predictability of Latin American machismo? Count on it. But we should do it anyway, for two reasons. First, the odds of a refugee terrorist attack may be very low, but the odds that an even-less-stable Middle East will produce terrorists or conflicts that will kill Americans is very high. Second, people usually remember you fondly when you bail them out of a tight spot, but the risk of blowback for slamming the door is huge. Between overthrowing all those governments, propping up other nasty ones, and uncompromising support for Israel no matter how many Palestinian olive groves they build houses on, we already have sufficient PR headaches in that region, and it's time for a win.

Speaking of winning, it's also time to play offense on behalf of the 3.3 million Muslims already in America. As liberals, our instinct is to defend all maligned minorities, but given how poorly that has been working, we need to start pointing out that the conservatives are offering nothing. So no more lectures about The Nation of Immigrants, no more bible verses about the Israelites in Egypt, and no more sticking our necks out for a group so large it's bound to include a few nutjobs. We need to take the hill in this fight and force conservatives to show their lousy hand.

Turn the tables by saying this: We know you don't like Muslims, and we think you spend far too much time fretting about them, but we're not here to tell you that you're wrong or racist. We're here to tell you that complaining about headscarves and blocking mosque construction at the local zoning board does not constitute a counter-terrorism strategy.

We're also here to tell you that your other ideas for fixing the situation don't work either. Military intervention? Seems like we've been there and done that. Travel ban? Even if it were legal and advisable, it would still be impossible. Religions, you may have noticed, don't issue passports or birth certificates. There's no master list of Muslims out there that border guards can cross reference.

And since we mentioned birth records, we should also point out that about one third of the Muslims in America were born here, so unless this brilliant non-plan includes deporting natural-born citizens, you'll just have to come with us as we attempt to figure out what's up with young loner men these days and what we can do about it. Really seems like one of those super tough problems that calls for some bipartisan teamwork, so we'll see you and your thinking caps at the meeting tomorrow. Don't be late, and if some the participants are wearing headscarves, please try not to point and stare.

This is not as satisfying an argument to make as some other liberal-for-conservative-reasons tent revival sessions we've been having. When it comes to stopping a violent invisible social contagion that infects very few people, we barely know where to start. In the best case scenario, we'll try a lot of things, the problem will go away, and then we'll spend a lot of time arguing about which one of those things actually did the trick. Or we'll just move on and find something more interesting to fight about.

The refugee issue is particularly frustrating. If you're not moved by helping people in need, helping refugees brings no obvious benefit other than avoiding future unseen problems. It's tough to get motivated by future unseen problems, which is why we don't use enough sunscreen, practice good posture, or save nearly enough for retirement. The whole business also has a bit of a lesser-of-two-evils flavor, and the warnings about future blowback may be real, but they also sound a bit like blackmail.

Dealing with a far-away refugee crisis turns out to be the geopolitical equivalent of fixing a slow-leaking pipe under the house: You know ignoring it will come to no good, and you know you have to fix it, but it's messy under the house and there are a lot of spiders. When you're done, the fix just sits down there, invisible, so you can't look at it and remind yourself of what a great crack plumber you are.

Still, it beats the hell out of the hear-no-evil, see-no-evil "strategy" of pretending that there's no risk at all. If moderates or conservatives are not getting what they want from the travel-ban-headscarf-freakout wing, they should be able to find something more on the left than a bunch of people who desperately want to believe that terrorism inspired by Islam, no matter what kooky and outside-the-mainstream interpretation we're dealing with here, is not actually a thing. They don't want to hear that this very real possibility that they see on TV all the time is something that only racists worry about, and they do not want the possibility of a difficult cultural clash dismissed as something that will work itself out as quickly as it does on Sesame Street.

People who value security above all else are more likely to respect arguments that address those concerns than arguments that center on people they don't know and don't care about. If we can make the case that helping refugees makes America a safer country, we might just bring enough conservatives on board to the idea of spending some money and getting used to a few more fresh faces stateside. They may think of it as the least-worst option, but they'll take it anyway, even if it's a liberal one.

PETER RICE

Chapter Five

_____

Underdogs, Excel charts, and why people don't really mind foreign trade.

BY THE TENDER AGE OF 16, I was well accustomed to the constant push and pull that is the gradual relaxation of the parental police state, and I flatter myself that I played the game fairly well. But opportunity knocked in a big, game-changing way that year, 1999, when for some inexplicable reason my parents allowed me to spend three days, by myself, at a major meeting of the World Trade

Organization in Seattle, covering the festivities on behalf of a college radio station I had been volunteering at. (You can probably infer from all this that I had a fairly unique childhood, but don't let that distract you from the big freedom deal this represented.)

Unbeknownst to us, this meeting, and the massive protest marches and general anarchy surrounding it, turned out to be the high water mark of the (mostly leftist) anti-globalization movement. Those three days prominently featured property destruction, clouds of tear gas, jittery cops arresting people for dumb reasons later laughed out of court, people dressed up as turtles, women wearing nothing from the waist up save electrical tape, less interesting but more massive and totally peaceful marches, and lots of cliche chants that started with "hey hey, ho ho" and ended with something sinister having to go.

Everybody who was anybody on the liberal fringe turned up for this one. I interviewed professional protester Medea Benjamin (now of Code Pink), followed Michael Moore and his camera crew around for a half hour, and attended a talk by the Indian scholar/activist Vandana Shiva. Future presidential spoiler (maybe) Ralph Nader and Teamster President James Hoffa were also traipsing around town giving speeches and rallying the faithful against this "globalization" thing and the scarily acronymed institution (the WTO) that represented it. They called it a threat to national sovereignty, worker rights, workers themselves, good wages, and the environment. They especially enjoyed pointing to factories in the midwest and rust belt that had closed and set up shop in Mexico as evidence of this global menace.

Bumbling around the downtown area, often blocked from their duties by the mayhem, was a small army of trade delegates from around the world, and while some responded to interview requests by insisting they were just tourists (if that was true, they were setting a new and very expensive standard for business formal clothing in the tourist class), a couple others were happy to point out that it was pretty rich for all this hot air against global trade to be emanating from a state completely dependent on it. The natural deepwater port in Seattle had been a catalyst for globalization since at least the Klondike gold rush 100 years before, and the little mom-and-pop aircraft shop known as Boeing was not about to limit itself to the domestic market.

And so our protagonist, a 16-year-old fledgling journalist, traipsed around a major left coast urban center with a microphone and tape recorder, taking note on the chaos, phoning reports back to the radio station mothership, dodging clouds of tear gas (with limited success), and at one point experiencing the thrill that is a riot cop pointing a menacing looking rubber bullet gun at your chest and yelling "stay back" (I did). The stuff of Mom's nightmares, to be sure, but my dream come true.

The week brought two main takeaways. First, it's very difficult to tell your son that he can't experience some new freedom after he has safely navigated an event informally called the "Battle in Seattle." (Seriously, I rode that precedent right up to the departure for college that rendered the whole business moot.) Second, trade and globalization may be the most hopelessly confused issue on the American political landscape.

Think about this: Tens of thousands of people turned up to protest at a meeting where mostly anonymous technocrats tried to hammer out the rules under which people from different countries exchange things for money. Scintillating topics under this umbrella include how much import or export tax one country can impose on another's stuff, what exactly counts as an illegal state support of a particular industry, and what to do if someone violates these rules.

If you're still awake, you should know that global trade bodies like these also spend a lot of time defining which goods belong in which tax categories. A metric ton of tee-shirts, for example, may be taxed at one rate, but a metric ton of tee-shirt discards destined for the shredder and a new life as some other product may be taxed at a completely different rate. Lots of people actually make a living figuring this stuff out, and if that seems like a fun career, you should probably fire off your resume to the WTO as soon as you finish reading this book. Far from a dull pastime, it would appear to be one of the more badass gigs on the planet, at least according to the protesters. They conflated this cadre of exceptionally boring people writing reports about tee-shirts with "The Man" and all that is wrong with the world, and saw the institution's existence as a fine reason to smash in a few windows at Nike Town.

That, or something else entirely was going on.

Anti-globalization activists, whether bubbling up in the form of leftists dressed as turtles in 1999, Pat Buchanan's various presidential campaigns before that, or our current administration in 2017, are not against trade, per se. They're perfectly fine with trading their money for groceries at the local grocery store. Ordering something from another state is also totally cool (even though, a measly couple of hundred years ago, that was basically considered international trade and might have involved the use of multiple currencies). And while a few people will talk a good game about supporting local businesses, they're probably not losing much sleep over the origins of the phone in their pocket, the coffee in the pantry, or even the car in the garage (which was probably made in several different countries). They probably also like knowing that they can fly to basically any place on earth and use their Visa debit card to acquire some local money that they can then spend at a shop where the clerk probably speaks at least some English. If you probed further and asked if it might make some sense for the various parties that make all these goods and services to come together and set up a few ground rules, they would probably shrug and wonder why you were asking a question with such an obvious answer. And if all that doesn't count as an endorsement of globalization, I don't know what does.

What these people are actually against is underdogs getting screwed and the massive disruption (and in some cases, devastation) that global trade can cause. Capitalism has always created winners and losers, and if you and your small business or large factory lose, it's not something that can be gotten over quickly, characters in Ayn Rand novels notwithstanding. If you lose to another country because they have lax environmental regulations or workplace safety rules or pay people $.30 an hour with no benefits, it's harder still to get over it. If that job was your plan A, B, and C because it's the only real game in your small town where your entire extended family and support network lives, it's even worse.

So whether you're concerned about the workers here at home, the workers in other countries, or the habitats destroyed by that lax regulation, there's plenty of bipartisan hatred to go around. Add to this the normal fear of large institutions that only seem to be completely understood by comfortable people with doctorates, subscriptions to the *Financial Times*, and a knack for Excel chart making, and it's no wonder people get angry.

In theory, of course, things turn out much better. The economists explaining comparative advantage tell us that trade is great because if everyone (or every country) focuses on what they can do most efficiently and then trades for everything else they need, everyone will be better off. So, the theory goes, Washington should focus on apples and Georgia should focus on peaches, then use the cash they get exporting all over the place to get what they don't have. If the two states tried to grow both crops, the theory continues, it would mean more effort going into less output, so everybody would be poorer.

Glancing over the elegant chart in the macroeconomics textbook (where the example usually, for some bizarre reason, involves guns and butter), it all makes perfect sense. And to be fair, it does actually work in the real world as well. But it quickly runs into a roadblock called human emotional response, something economists have always had a tough time illustrating in Excel. So goes the debate over global trade: Some 53-year-old in Ohio loses basically the only job he has ever had or is likely to get, and the free trade advocates say, "don't worry – take a look at this chart," then go back to their comfortable lives.

Predictably, that 53-year-old, who was really hoping to just make it to 65 and call it a career, is not quite in the mood at that point to vote for nuance-oriented politicians who will thoroughly pore over the basically sensible trading rules and perhaps make a few modifications to subsection d, paragraph six, thus hopefully discouraging the future flight of factories to other countries or otherwise helping displaced workers. Not a chance. This guy just had his life burned down, and he would, in turn, like to ruin the life of whomever was playing with the matches. There's a direct line between that sentiment and the president nixing the Trans Pacific Partnership while unnerving the hell out of our largest trading partners. It's also why a country that on the whole benefits massively from international trade is suddenly against it.

I don't mean to brag, but my 16-year-old self called it there on the streets of Seattle in 1999: If this small group of people over here, I thought, continues pissing off the large group of people over there, we'll eventually get some serious blowback. It was hardly a revolutionary observation, and I'm sure some of the "tourists" had the same thought. What they did not have was the wherewithal to take it slow and offer a little help to the voting blocs worth of economic losers they would help create.

Trade is not really a liberal or conservative thing, and I confess some of the premise of the book breaks down on this issue. Buchanan carried the torch for a while, then passed it to the the environmentalists and trade unions. Ralph Nader sniffed at it and Bernie Sanders picked it up in a big way, only to be eclipsed by another presidential candidate who has, paradoxically enough, done quite a bit of international trade personally. Now that the liberal party is the home of the urban wealthy people who do great under the global trade order (Hillary won Orange County, a distinction she shares with no other modern Democratic candidate except Franklin Roosevelt.), it's anybody's guess how the sides will shift next.

But again, trade is not really what we're talking about. People basically like it, and it's backed by the most powerful people in society, so I'm pretty optimistic that it will do fine in the long run. This is really just about the people who worked in industries hammered by international trade (and in many other cases we probably don't talk about enough, automation) who are now extremely pissed off.

Six years after the WTO meeting, I got to see something of this phenomenon at my first job out of college, as a general assignment reporter in an extremely rural county of about 20,000 people on the southern Oregon coast. It's a blue state, of course, but like most rural areas, Curry County is as red as a stop sign. They voted for Dole in 1996, Bush in 2000, and just before I arrived, Bush again in 2004. They haven't come close to voting Democratic since.

The traditional economy of the Oregon coast involves cutting down trees in the abundant forests and taking fish out of the ocean and rivers. The jobs were tough, dangerous, and dirty, but they paid very well, didn't require a lot of formal education, and kept a lot of men happily occupied for a long time. The reasons why most of those jobs went away are complex, but a very simple explanation had permeated all coastal conversation mills and became something of an article of faith. The official line, parroted even by the few Democrats that could be found there, was that the federal government shut down logging on public lands in the 1990s because they cared more about the endangered Northern Spotted Owl than human beings, and a similar crackdown on fishing was well underway for equally dumb reasons.

This was obviously not the fault of some corporation pulling up stakes and moving to Mexico. It had nothing to do with one robot doing the job thirty people used to do. But the results were the same, and today, dire conditions are not hard to find. The largest of the three incorporated municipalities in the county, Brookings, actually enjoys a poverty rate of about 10 percent, below the national average of 15 percent, according to Census data. But cross the Chetco River, to the unincorporated town of Harbor, and the rate climbs to 28 percent. To the north, the county seat of Gold Beach is at 20 percent, and further north, the city of Port Orford stands at 36 percent.

The counterintuitive part of the story is that all things considered, Curry County wasn't then and today isn't actually doing so badly. Commercial fishing still employs a fair number of people. So do logging and one surviving local mill. And the Oregon coast is exceptionally beautiful, which attracts a steady stream of tourists, especially those interested in sport fishing. Sport fishermen are really quite bad at fishing when you get right down to it, and in the process of barely catching anything they happily spend thousands of dollars on hotels, meals, and gear, so that's a local economic win. Meanwhile, a bunch of Californians were selling their homes at the height of the bubble, moving north where they could buy something bigger for half the price, and driving up real estate prices up in the process. So the old timers who had bought in back in the day at least had a nest egg they could count on.

Really, a lot of people were doing just fine, thank you very much. Childhood poverty today stands at 25 percent, and 61 percent of kids in school are eligible for free and reduced lunch, according to Kids Count data from the Casey Foundation. That may be terrible, but Multnomah County, which includes Portland and gave 76 percent of its vote to Hillary Clinton, is at a 23 percent poverty rate and 53 percent for the lunch – not revolutionarily better off.

Closer to my current home, the poverty rate of extremely rural Rio Arriba County in northern New Mexico is much worse than Curry's, with a 30 percent child poverty rate and at least 70 percent of school kids on free lunch, according to state data. And they voted for Clinton with 64 percent. Bill even came to visit – not for the first time – and was warmly received.

Plenty of places have had some recent economic upheaval that was worse than what Curry went through. Rio Arriba County was worse off during Curry's boom and is still worse off during Curry's (somewhat deceptive) bust. So what gives?

What gives is that people are not rational. If politics were a game of showing fundamentally calm people the right numbers on a chart, we would have solved this problem a long time ago. The thing Curry

County has in common with the former factory towns in states that actually elected the president is a very recent, very intense psychological humiliation. We had jobs, the story goes – good ones that we worked hard at. But *they* took them away from *us*. Now, *we* are forced to take *their* public assistance or participate as submissive pawns in *their* service economy (decidedly unmasculine jobs).

The humiliated are left with only a collection of stories about the houses and cars they could once afford, and some aging pieces of public infrastructure built when they were flush, from city hall in Brookings, to the paved road up the Rogue River to the tiny hamlet of Agness. Meanwhile, the insults continue to rain down from above: The feds do throw the old timber counties some crumbs of money to make up for the lack of logging, but it's always a long and protracted fight, and each twist and turn in the legislative reauthorization process is another reminder that a once proud people are reduced to asking the government for money. And it's not enough anyway.

Every so often, a small reason for hope pops into the news – generally some rumor that a logging or fishing regulation will be relaxed. Like a hungry street kid looking into the window of a bakery, there is a brief, pleasant daydream of hope, and a swift and crushing return to reality. Each step of this torturous process serves as a loud reminder that America's political power is drifting toward cities, where the people view rural areas as hopelessly unsophisticated backwaters at worst, and at best, nice places to visit on the weekend and then ignore.

It's hard to illustrate the community-wide trauma such a situation can bring. You can't really see it by walking down the street and you won't generally read about it in the papers I used to help produce. But the story – the unresolved issue – dominates the county's psychology nonetheless. That school board member may appear to be just patiently reviewing the latest dismal budget projections, asking appropriate and professional questions, but just below the surface is the thought that "this didn't use to be a problem before *they* did this to *us.*" Similar thought processes dominate other community leaders and normal citizens alike. If you're just passing through town to stay at the nice hotel on the beach or stroll around the cute shops, they may not mention it. But if you're an outsider reporter paid to listen, they're happy to talk. Those who feel themselves to be invisible, unwanted, and forgotten will think of nothing else, and then they vote.

We as a country thought we could ignore these people, but that didn't work very well, so a liberal solution for conservative reasons is in order: Very simply, we should do way, way more for them. Not for annoying humanitarian motives, of course. We should help them because if we don't they might continue to screw up our best-laid plans to get rich by selling stuff to people in foreign countries.

We should also help them, and promote trade, because even the lousiest student of history will tell you that open warfare is probably the most frightening thing humans are capable of and we should take great pains to avoid it. Trading with all comers creates millions of transnational relationships, large and small, and a massively powerful anti-war constituency. If open war with a big trading partner ever looms, you can bet thousands of CEOs will be calling up the White House to complain and make threats about campaign contributions, and that is a fantastically great thing. Trading partners tend to not fight with each other at all, but if they do, it looks like a bunch of lawyers writing very dull letters. Run that scenario by one of the few remaining veterans of World War II, and I bet they'll tell you it's a slam dunk win for everybody.

But when a factory or lumber mill closes and the bottom falls out of a town, we only seem to hear big talk. We hear about retraining programs for displaced workers, or about efforts to lure in some new factory that never seem to quite succeed (or if they do, the factory involves a lot of robots and not too many humans). We hear about the unemployment benefits, disability benefits, food stamps, and other programs which people will take in a pinch but which do not actually constitute solutions. The global economy being what it is, this sort of disruption happens faster and faster in less predictable ways. Layoffs are painful in the bigger cities, but at least there are more Plan B options available. In smaller, more rural, and more isolated areas, the big talk doesn't pan out nearly enough, and all of the above aside, these politically weak communities are pretty much left to fend for themselves. Check back five or ten years later, and it usually hasn't gone well. Even when it goes sort of okay, as with Curry County, the situation is still economically and socially corrosive.

And no rational observer would expect otherwise. Humans are pretty adaptable, but it's asking too much to expect hundreds or thousands of people to roll with that kind of punch. The young, the flexible, and the clever may leave town and find great jobs elsewhere. Others will take all that retraining aid and put it to good use, finding some new job in the new economy. But some people are older and don't know what else to do. Others are just less resourceful, or have too many local family connections or other social support systems to contemplate starting life over again in a new town. Selling a house to raise cash for a move is suddenly much harder, in any event. Local governments, meanwhile, find themselves managing the same infrastructure with no tax base and a shrinking population. Abandoned houses breed crime, brain drains deplete the local political talent pool, and a general air of hopelessness and anger diminishes the social fabric. The buildup to the boom is wondrously heady but the decline is long and depressing.

What if, instead of the last few decades worth of empty talk in former factory, logging, and mining towns, the state and federal government had parachuted in and offered displaced workers some real options. Lots of help going back to school and starting a new career would still be on the menu, with perhaps more emphasis on moving to a boom area if that's at all possible. But beyond that, why couldn't the government also buy up homes at pre-bust prices, giving residents a nice dowry they could use to start a new life elsewhere? The house would probably end up demolished, but an empty field deeded over to the local municipality is better than an untended den for vagrants and crime.

For those who are more-or-less stuck in the community, there's an even more simple solution, one we were happy to use when this degree of economic devastation was affecting the whole country: Make them a job. At that big, tense high school gym meeting where people try to digest the catastrophe, find the 53-year olds with kids who can't imagine any other life and tell them: "Congratulations: You now work for the Forest Service and we have some trails that need building." Or, "Congratulations: We're going to pay your city government to hire you to spruce up the local park, or repave Main Street, or dig a new fiber-optic line, manage some project, or crunch numbers for any one of those efforts. Some people could even work remotely.

We haven't really done that sort of thing since F.D.R. And sure, it's uncomfortable to contemplate and even worse to administer, but would it really be so wrong? The free market, bolstered by efficient education and relocation programs, will take care of part of the devastation it creates – hopefully a large part. But it won't do anybody any good to let the problem cases that remain fester for decades. We know who these people are. Just give them something productive to do, something they can be proud of, something they can show off to visiting relatives, something that might even make the community attractive enough for the industries of tomorrow. Match their old salary and benefits, and keep 'em on until they decide to move or retire. Of course, don't do it forever. The next generation will have to figure out a new plan, maybe in a new place, but they'll have sufficient advanced warning to make it happen.

Liberals for liberal reasons would do it because they want to believe we're a compassionate society that does its best not to leave people behind and doesn't concern itself with cold free market orthodoxy in emergency situations. Besides being annoying, this asks people to care about other people they don't know who live in places they don't identify with. Many of the people being asked to care would happily throw around terms like "white trash" to describe the people they're being asked to care about, which does not seem like a good foundation for success.

Liberals for conservative reasons only ask that you care about yourself. For our own sake, we had better do something because ignoring this problem will not make it go away, and we'll be forced to deal with it eventually. The challenge of figuring out how to pay for the post-catastrophe bailout is small potatoes next to the opioid addiction epidemic we'll have to deal with later when the social fabric collapses. Besides, the long-term, multigenerational welfare dependency we're encouraging by doing nothing might well be more expensive than all the short-term spending.

Most of all, we should send help because inaction creates mobs of unhappy, desperate people who will happily vent their frustration by voting for any two-bit orange-haired snake oil salesman carnival barker who comes down the damn pike. Liberals and international business tycoons who like free trade had headaches for different reasons that terrible morning last November, but they both hurt just as bad and should be avoided in the future.

Political fights about trade are not really about trade at all. People like trade. They even like international trade. What they don't like is being left out in the cold without any prospects, humiliated. Assuming the current regime fails to help, liberals and their pro-trade conservative allies may one day soon have an opening to do what F.D.R. did: Shave off a few of capitalism's rough edges in a few places so it can thrive everywhere else. That way we can continue a global trade order that is not only the best hope we've got for peace in our time, but can also, on balance, make us filthy stinking rich.

PETER RICE

Chapter Six

_____

Essential healthcare, free stuff, and why birth control concerns us all.

FIFTY YEARS AFTER THE FDA APPROVED the first oral contraceptive pill, you could be forgiven for thinking the controversy was pretty well over. Family sizes plummeted, people waited longer to have kids, more people chose not to have kids at all, and we all seemed to be pretty okay with that. People voted, if not exactly with their feet, and a thorough counting of the ballots revealed that birth control won. Even overwhelming majorities of

Catholics now just smile and nod and ignore whatever the church has to say on the matter.

Turns out, however, the long war had one more battle left to fight, and it came on that golden anniversary year, in 2010, when Congress passed the Affordable Care Act (more commonly known as Obamacare). The bill itself barely mentioned contraceptives, but it did spell out a broad framework for a new, generally more comprehensive definition of health insurance, including lots of preventative medicine extras that all had to be included in basically every plan issued in the country without any – and here are the magic words – "cost sharing."

That's health insurance speak for "you've already paid for it." In other words, they can't charge you an extra co-payment or other fee for that preventative medicine. Just keep paying your monthly premium, and you're good. Nobody paid much attention to this until long after the bill had passed Congress, when the government finally spelled out what those preventative extras would be. It turned out to be a boring mixture of vaccinations and screenings, plus one revolutionary ingredient: birth control.

This delighted liberals, of course, because they are in favor of, well, liberal dispensation of healthcare. They had been carrying the birth control access banner for a long time, and telling health plans that it had come standard at no extra cost was a huge victory. On the other side, the move at first didn't seem to galvanize conservatives quite as much as religious conservatives. Religiously affiliated institutions, especially Catholic ones, didn't much care for the new mandate, preferring to pay their employees in the form of money that they could pretend would not be spent on birth control. Litigation ensued, and any hope that this issue would go quietly into the night vanished.

The matter played out in the courts, but it was also worked over quite a bit in the public square, with liberals once again arguing talking points designed to appeal to the smallest possible audience. This was about women's health, they said, and women's control over their own bodies (in an echo of the abortion debate we'll tackle next). Whether birth control coverage is available, they continued, should not be up to the capriciousness or religious preference of their employer.

Conservatives tend to see birth control as an optional health-related lifestyle choice you're free to make if you pay for it – hardly a surprise from the side that trends older, more male, and more laissez faire. And since it's relatively cheap, at least as healthcare goes, they think it shouldn't be something that we have to put into standardized health plans that effectively spread the costs to everyone, including people who don't need birth control, like men and older women.

The talk of women's health and control fell flat in camp conservative because of the reality that not a few women had somehow figured out birth control long before the government mandate came around. They suspected that this discussion was actually code for buying birth control for irresponsible people who couldn't get their act together, which is never fun. And the line about employers didn't work because the mandate itself was brand new at the time. All those employers that had optionally covered birth control up until ten minutes ago were not going to suddenly become omniscient gatekeepers deciding whether you could get it at all.

Round about this time, conservatives also deftly turned "zero cost sharing" into "free," so even though this birth control is about as free as the breakfast at Hampton Inn, they could now spin it as a bunch of women wanting the government to subsidize their sex lives. Which was clever of them, if nothing else.

Liberals couldn't help but notice an anti-female bias in all this. Isn't it interesting, they thought, how nobody seemed to give a rip about the zero-cost-sharing flu shots and various other screenings, including those for predominately male prostate cancer, but all of a sudden when preventative healthcare involves women and sex, it's her problem. When liberals notice enough things like that, they suddenly feel quite comfortable dropping the "war on women" bomb into the conversation, a gratifying and unhelpful catharsis.

And so, the birth control fight became a fight about women. The liberals for liberal reasons said it was about all women, specifically those of childbearing age, and the conservatives said it was about irresponsible women who should manage their money better and pay for their own birth control without whining to the government for help.

All this, of course, distracted everyone from the fundamental insanity of the argument. Birth control certainly involves women, but it's really about society, which includes not a few men (many of whom, incidentally, are very much concerned about birth control) and women not of childbearing age. Liberals for liberal reasons worked tirelessly to shrink the appeal of this issue to the smallest voting bloc possible, but liberals for conservative reasons will go for an actual winning majority.

Let's start with what we all agree on: Lots of people out there are not even close to being ready for childrearing primetime. Maybe they're totally broke, totally irresponsible, totally unstable, totally addicted to something terrible, or totally 15 years old – the reason doesn't really matter. People like that are not likely to have their financial planning act together enough to be on high quality, long-term birth control. That means they're more likely to have kids and do a terrible job raising them.

And soon enough, that becomes a problem we can't hide from. Unwanted kids raised by unqualified parents are very likely to end up in welfare programs, prisons, and psychiatric hospitals that we all have to pay for. They're more likely to have problems with addiction, which means they're more likely to break into your house and steal stuff they can sell to get more drugs. And even if they stay on this side of the law, they're likely to have all kinds of problems getting along with others, which will hold back progress in classrooms your children are trying to learn in and cause you headaches when they become adults and get hired on at your job.

Of course, it would be great if everyone had their financial and logistical act together enough to figure out their own birth control without making it a matter of public concern. And as long as we're dreaming, I'd like a million dollars, a private jet, and someone with a British accent to fly me around while saying things like "jolly good, sir." But back in reality, they don't have it together, a fact conservatives have clearly noticed, judging by how much time they spend ranting about stupid poor people having too many kids.

Rage will not bring the tax dollars back, and this unwanted kid problem is way too important and way too long-term expensive to leave to chance. So by all means, let's make sure nobody has to pay anything extra to get contraceptives, including those more expensive implant devices that are very effective and last several years. Let's go one step further and let pharmacies distribute whatever birth control they reasonably can, without a prescription – or give pharmacists themselves limited prescription powers in this area. Let's make every Wal-Mart, Walgreens, and CVS in this great land a one-stop, no-extra-cost birth control shop – like the model they already use for the flu shot. While we're at it, they should be able to figure out how to bill insurance even if you don't have your card handy, and if applicable, without parents finding out.

If we aggressively promote free birth control, everybody wins, and there's no argument about that. Colorado ran a six-year experiment that gave out free (really free – not 'zero cost sharing') long-term birth control like candy at community health clinics. By 2013, the teen pregnancy rate was down 48 percent, far outpacing a similarly heartening national trend in that direction. The teen abortion rate went down by the same percentage. The experiment cost $25 million but saved the government an estimated $66 million worth of budget for Medicaid and various other assistance programs, according to the state's Department of Public Health. These are the kind of cost savings that should have conservatives cracking huge smiles.

The more we make access to birth control a "woman" thing bolstered by talking points that basically only liberal women of reproductive age identify with, the more we confine this critical issue to a dark corner with no political power. That's way too risky. We didn't get to this happy place of no-extra-cost birth control because of some massive political upwelling that the new Republican government can't ignore. We got it because the Obama administration backed it into a health law that is not likely to be on stable ground over the next few years, the Republican's initial failure to repeal it notwithstanding.

Saving it won't be easy, but we'll have better luck defending it like a liberal for conservative reasons, because this is way beyond a women's issue. It saves tax money and improves every social institution we have, government and otherwise. If we fail to keep what we have and build on it, the only irresponsible idiots we'll have left to rage at are ourselves.

LIBERAL FOR CONSERVATIVE REASONS

PETER RICE

Chapter Seven

Abortion and the fight for the nuanced middle.

IT MAY BE JAW-DROPPINGLY BIZZARE that we're still fighting over birth control, but given the wide popularity of the product itself, the beachhead represented by the Affordable Care Act, and the fact that amongst millennials, the debate is won and done, the long-term smart money is probably on the liberal side. One day soon, it will mostly likely take its rightful place in the winners wing of the culture war hall of fame, right there next to gay marriage.

Abortion, not so much.

Conventional wisdom holds that, as of this writing, a one-vote majority on the Supreme Court will uphold Roe v. Wade, down from two votes during the era of Justice Sandra Day O'Connor. About 30 states stand ready to outlaw the procedure should Roe fall.

The opinion of the American public doesn't seem to be much different. According to Pew, a narrow majority supports legal abortion in most or all circumstances. But in the time that gay marriage went from a fanciful and outlandish practice in the Netherlands to the widely-accepted law of this land, opinions on abortion haven't moved much at all. There's not much reason to suspect that demographic changes will sweep us to a resolution either. Liberals aren't exactly losing, but they ought to feel very uncomfortable.

The pro-abortion-rights side, meanwhile, wraps itself in the rhetoric of choice. This is about women having control over their bodies, they say, just like with contraception. It should be a personal decision made in consultation with a medical professional, and not needlessly hampered by cumbersome regulations about mandatory ultrasounds, waiting periods, or parental notifications.

The anti-abortion side, of course, responds with a two-word argument: killing babies. Which, if nothing else, efficiently gets to the point.

The pro-abortion rights side might go a little deeper and talk about how ultimate control over fertility really makes women full citizens. After all, if you're one accident, one poorly planned drunken evening, or one violent attack away from a pregnancy that could derail a career, make it hard to leave town, and saddle you with an enormous medical, financial, and time commitment (ready or not), you're not exactly equal with the guys in the picture, since in many cases they get away without further involvement.

And countering this, the anti-abortion side repeats the baby-killing line, because they are nothing if not consistent. There might be some side comment about needing to think about that responsibility sometime before getting pregnant, but mostly the whole baby killing thing seems to check the argument box for them.

And so, like most controversial issues, the two sides talk past each other. One side makes the autonomy and equality of women the top moral priority because they genuinely believe it is. The other side makes the bodily integrity of unborn babies the top moral priority, and they genuinely believe in that, too. Where you stand depends on where you sit, and the two sides sit in very different moral places, with basically no room for compromise. Nobody who spends all their time thinking about the equal place of women in society is going to be persuaded by people who think even a few cells under a microscope constitute a human being. And nobody who is convinced that abortion is cold-blooded murder will be moved by arguments about it not being the right time to have a baby. But we digress into old news.

What's interesting about this generally depressing debate is not that the two sides are talking past each other, but the vast canyon of more nuanced public opinion over which they must shout. According to Gallup, about 20 percent of us think abortion should be illegal in all circumstances, and according to your author, it's safe to assume that includes the usual suspects from Operation Rescue, the National Right to Life Committee, and the Family Research Council. Meanwhile, about 30 percent of us think it should be legal in all circumstances, and it seems equally safe to assume that this includes the crews from NARAL Pro-Choice America, the National Abortion Federation, and the National Organization for Women. But about 50 percent of us, says Gallup, think abortion should be legal "only under certain circumstances." That's a very big group of people and a very poorly defined opinion.

The only thing that's safe to say about this cohort is that they are not driving the debate. Lots of factors seem to influence their take on abortion, including the health of the mother, the life of the mother, whether a woman is asking the poll question, whether the pregnancy was caused by rape or incest, and of course, the particular trimester in question. It's easy to conjure up some hypothetical person who is turned off both by the cavalier attitudes of the pro-choice side, real or imagined, *and* the fundamentalist attitudes of the pro-life side. You can think ill of the lowlifes who display big pictures of mangled fetuses all over town and also think ill of late term abortion. Or maybe that late term abortion would be okay in the right set of circumstances. Maybe "my body my choice" doesn't resonate, but some poverty stricken 16-year-old walking into a clinic does. Maybe you're totally anti-abortion except for the life and (get ready for a squishy term) health of the mother. Maybe you are just generally squicked out by abortion, more in the late term, but not so much early on, but a specific case with the right circumstances could throw all that out the window.

You wouldn't know it from listening to the public debate, but for once, it seems, a plurality of Americans have settled for dozens of different shades of gray rather than an either-or proposition. And that hasn't changed much since the mid-70s, when Roe v. Wade was decided.

But shades of gray do not a political movement make, if only because you can never fit all those caveats on the signs. It's also difficult to actually write legislation for a group that almost seems to prefer approaching everything on a case-by-case basis. And so the debate rages on, liberals spend more and more political capital on defense, and a large group of America is left without much of a political home. Liberals for liberals reasons will no doubt keep trying to grow their 30 percent share of public opinion, but since that number has barely budged in 40 years, it seems time for a new strategy.

The liberal-for-conservative-reasons prescription is to make a home for the 50 percent, one that is closely aligned with the goals of the left, but not the rhetoric. Call it pro-choice for pro life reasons: Acknowledge the tragic element that nobody on team choice wants to talk about, establish doubt about the efficacy of banning or restricting abortion, then offer real strategies for reducing the abortion rate. Whether it's the traditional pro-choice community making this pitch or some third way group, it's long-overdue.

The tragic element: Lots of people out there are nowhere near joining a picket line at the local Planned Parenthood, and support abortion rights in at least some circumstances, but that doesn't mean they're not unnerved, saddened, or even disgusted by the procedure. This third way movement needs to make clear that these thoughts are okay to think and that the thinker is not alone. The pro-choice side likes to medicalize abortion with talk of "terminating pregnancies" and even "abortion care," but this is not exactly a trip to the dentist and we all know it. Most people feel relief, but sometimes people feel sad or regretful. This is totally normal. But don't take my word for it: Those last two sentences are quoted directly from an FAQ for patients on the Planned Parenthood website. It is a tough issue, and if they can say it out loud, everybody can.

The doubt: We need to make it clear that banning abortion, or putting up roadblocks like waiting periods or parental consent, is both the least effective way to reduce the abortion rate and the most effective way to kill women. Restrict it all you want, or ban it outright, and people with determination or money or both will still be able to go to a blue state or, if push comes to shove, another country. The abortion pill is now well established and wouldn't be too hard to administer away from the prying eyes of authorities. Sympathetic doctors were there before Roe and would be there after as well. From there, it's home remedies, quacks, coat hangers, and stuff ordered off black market internet pharmacies. It gets really ugly really fast. Sure, a few more poor women without access to good transportation or helpful social networks will end up carrying pregnancies to term. But if the pre-Roe experience is any guide, hundreds or thousands of women will probably end up getting themselves killed every year in the process of achieving this "victory," and that price is too high.

Real strategies: We know how to reduce the abortion rate and help women at the same time (to say nothing of the rest of society). It's as simple as the easiest possible access to the most effective, longest-term birth control that money can buy. But there's a lot to do, starting with the fight over the Affordable Care Act's birth control mandate discussed in the previous chapter. We've already discussed how we can pitch easy access to zero-extra-cost birth control at every pharmacy as a win for taxpayers, but we can just as easily pitch it as a great way to lower the abortion rate. That will appeal to the lean-pro-life faction, and it might even bring some of them on board to the idea of expanding that easy birth control availability to people without health insurance.

Best of all, we know this will work. The abortion rate has been tanking in recent years, and is actually lower today than it was when Roe was decided. This is either because of (1.) new restrictions on abortion in our least populated states or least populated parts of states like Texas, (2.) a sudden outbreak of chastity in America that nobody seems to have noticed, or (3.) widespread adoption of the sort of highly effective long-term birth control described in the last chapter.

This is not a new way to think about abortion. Bill Clinton probably best summed up an appeal to the vast nuanced middle with his pronouncement that abortion should be "safe, legal, and rare." It was an olive branch if not for the pro-life side, then to those who kind of maybe lean that way. (Lots of liberals hate the "rare" part because it allegedly stigmatizes abortion, but they should review the vote count on the Supreme Court and ask themselves if we can afford the hard line on this one.) We came to expect nothing less from the center-left ex-governor of a conservative state. But somewhere along the way, we retreated back into the tribal cocoon, and left about half of America politically homeless.

Writing off the people not in you club is rarely a safe exercise. We may be able to get away with ignoring tiny minorities, like the folks who want to break off parts of southern Oregon and Northern California to form a new state called Jefferson (true story). Or vegans. But writing off half of America as hopelessly anti-women, for perhaps supporting parental consent laws or some other idea that sounds reasonable but isn't, doesn't make the future of legal abortion less precarious.

Some of this 50 percent are more friend than foe, and we need to keep them close. The rest are potential enemies, and we need to keep them closer. Because if these people look to the right and see obnoxious clinic picketers with gorey photos, then look to the left only to see people who don't seem to be even the least bit weirded out by abortion, there's no telling what they'll do. But if they look to the left and see not just the hardliners, but also a less fundamentalist group with a coherent and intuitive argument for safe and legal, plus some solid ideas on rare, abortion rights might just find, at long last, a secure future.

PETER RICE

Chapter Eight

Healthcare, health insurance, and why bankruptcy court is socialized medicine

AT FIRST GLANCE, this whole health care issue seems like it doesn't belong. We just finished two chapters that get into some pretty deep stuff – like the sanctity of life, sex, and religious traditions that have kept communities together for many a generation. When these things clash with rapid changes in medical technology and the rising political power of women, nobody is surprised when some fireworks go off. You can practically see that scientist back in the lab in the 1950s, developing the pill and thinking, "this one's gonna leave a wake."

But really? Healthcare finance? How many decades will we spend fighting over how to pay for this stuff? How many administrations must be consumed with the shockingly boring mechanics of doctors and hospitals? Somehow we maintain a standing army, an old age pension, Carlsbad Caverns National Park, the University of Montana, an interstate highway system, your local elementary school, and the sidewalks outside your house – and we manage this without constantly fighting about how to pay for it. Sure we make some adjustments here and there, feathers get ruffled, and grudges get formed, but by and large we have a system, we're used to it, and we're cool with it. If there is a group of activists ready to descend on congressional town hall meetings to demand a new way to pay for regular garbage collection, I am not aware of it.

Yet here we are, ploughing toward a new decade, still droning on.

Of course, at second glance, this dysfunctional melee of blithering nonsense that passes for a healthcare debate makes perfect sense. It's expensive as all hell, and it's only going to get worse, which always riles people up. Plus there's the matter of what to do with poor people, which turns it all into a welfare debate. Add to this mix the healthcare industrial complex, which is big and influential and would prefer to keep it that way, and – okay, fine. I get it.

But really, when you get right down to the origins of the problem, it's pretty simple. Humans, you see, get sick from time to time. Or they get injured. Not very often for most of us, and we hopefully consider ourselves lucky, but sooner or later, pretty much everyone gets into a tight medical spot. Depending on just how tight a spot we're talking about, the bill for the healthcare services you need could be somewhere between what you might spend on a moderately good night at a bar and what Anheuser-Busch might spend on hops and barley since its founding in 1852.

As you might guess, that presents something of a problem. When it comes to other human needs, such as food, we have a pretty good idea of what we'll be spending next week, and even a decade or two from now. Prices creep up with inflation, and once in awhile there's an egg or cacao shortage that causes some drama, but in general, nobody quakes in fear that one day they could wake up to a $100,000 grocery bill they weren't expecting.

Since very few of us have that kind of cash rolling around under the couch cushions (or a realistic capacity to save it), and since we're an ingenious and highly social type, we invented (drumroll please) health insurance. Actually, several different types of health insurance, but if you squint they're pretty much all the same: We pass the hat every so often, usually once or twice a month, and if you happen to get sick or injured you get the money. Which would be great, except that it inconveniently comes in the form of people in white lab coats telling you to take your pants off.

Sometimes a corporation called an insurance company partners with another corporation called your job and does all that periodic hat passing with all the employees and their families. With your retired parents and super poor people, the hat gets passed to everyone with a paycheck, and they throw in with a tax.

This was pretty much the end of the story for American health insurance, up until about 2010. But as you will recall, not all before then was peaches and cream and tongue depressors.

There were two main problems with the groups-passing-hats method of paying for the mother of all bar tabs mentioned above. First, doctors were increasingly not content to merely tell you to take your pants off. They found ways to detect and remove tumors, for instance, and they invented the triple bypass and the intensive care unit. Colleagues of theirs came up with gadgets that would shoot invisible particles at you as a way to see inside your body without breaking out the knives. Still others came up with a vaccine for shingles and the Ebola virus.

It was all well and good and impressive, but unfortunately all of these highly trained professionals expected to be paid handsomely for their work and for all the specialized tools and potions they were carting around. These achievements started to really pile up, and pretty soon if you came into a hospital with a heart attack, they could do quite a bit more than monitor your vital signs and hope for the best. Cancer treatment, once a very affordable process of watching people slowly die, became an actual and very expensive thing. Given that these medical professionals presently won't shut up about gene editing and stem cell therapy – whatever that is – it's safe to assume that this treadmill will get steeper and steeper. A few accountants and human resource officers are probably wistfully looking back through history to the days when "medicine" was just some dude with six months of training carrying a bag of leeches and python bile around town, but everyone else seems pretty happy that those days are behind us.

Side note: People yelling about healthcare politics almost never talk about this as a significant source of cost increases. Ask a liberal about prices, and you'll get a speech about greedy insurance companies siphoning off tons of money while contributing no value to the system, as if negotiating down rates with aggressive doctors and hospitals counts for nothing. Ask a conservative, and you'll get a speech about how free market competition will solve everything, usually ending with a nod to the crazy drop in the price of laser eye surgery. Which is great, but we still spent less on our eyes back when glasses were the only option. Also, the people paramedics scrape out of wrecked cars and take to the hospital are not generally in a position to call around and get three quotes.

In any event, this stuff eventually got so expensive that all those corporations, which had basically been putting lots of money into the hat on behalf of employees (then paying them less to make up for it), started telling people that they were going to have to chip in more and more of their own money. Governments that ran their own hat-passing schemes also took note, and started to worry. Some businesses abandoned the hat passing all together, with contributed to problem two.

Problem two had been sitting around for quite a while but nobody powerful enough ever managed to care. Basically, life was pretty okay if you were poor enough (Medicaid) or old enough (Medicare) for government-supported insurance. Life was also pretty okay if you worked for an employer big enough to have group insurance. But life was decidedly not okay for a group I'll call "everyone else," which included small business workers and owners, plus less telegenic poor-but-not-poor-enough people, many of whom were personally as dysfunctional as the larger system. For this lot, there were few good options, and that is mainly because of what happens every time anyone applies for any type of insurance as an individual or small group, without an army of buying power behind them.

By way of illustration, let's consider what happens when you try to sign up for the mandatory insurance hat-passing scheme that helps make whole the owner of the Kia Sorento you pasted into the other day. The auto insurance company, when you apply, is naturally quite curious to learn whether, in your illustrious driving career, you have left a trail of other Kia Sorentos in your wake. They would also appreciate knowing if alcohol was a factor in this or any other driving incident you've experienced. Finally, they try to get to know you personally (if not exactly in a friendly, neighborly sort of way), asking about such things as your gender, your age, where you live, and what sort of car you'll be driving with this insurance.

This is, of course, how they make money and stay in business. They assess risk, and charge accordingly, which is why 17-year-old boys pay through the nose, but when they later become 40-year-old men enjoying the bonds of holy matrimony (and quite possibly, a Kia Sorento), they pay much less. Once in awhile, someone with a few drunk driving arrests or some other pile of uninsurable issues gets booted off the plan, or never gets on in the first place, and that's what friends, bikes, buses, Uber, and legs are for.

You can see how trouble would crop up by using the same arrangement for healthcare. Thanks to those obnoxiously genius doctors and medical researchers innovating so much, the price of healthcare could be ruinous for an insurance company contracting with a mere one person or their nuclear family. Human bodies are more complex machines than cars, medical professionals make more than mechanics, and we dislike it immensely when doctors declare patients "totaled" for cost reasons and send them to the junkyard to be sold for spare parts (as cost efficient as that would be).

So the insurers, wishing to avoid bankruptcy, insured only the healthiest people they could find. If you had a health history, even a minor one, they might show you the door, or possibly write you a policy that excluded coverage for that particular item on your health resume. If you enrolled but later developed a health history, they might show you the door at that point, or raise your premiums substantially. Still others never got a chance to play because, despite being healthy, they didn't have the extra cash.

In short, while it was actually a pretty good deal for very healthy and reasonably affluent people with their act together, it didn't work so well for everyone else. There's not really a great Uber-like backup out there in the event that the health insurance system doesn't want to deal with you. And it's asking a lot for people in hospitality and the trades, dominated as they are by small businesses, to see if they can't just find a different career or a bigger company to work for. (Besides, who would tend bar?) Then there were all the poverty-stricken wretches out there, who were not exactly the face of the reform movement, but who nonetheless did not settle for the leech and python bile method when they got brutally sick, so we ended up paying for them anyway.

Some people managed to hack together workarounds, but about 15 percent of America couldn't, for whatever reason, get into one of the hat passing groups. So they kept on with life, hoping that their number would never come up. They paid for small stuff out of pocket or tried to get by with charity care, but if there was a big catastrophe, they flung themselves at the nearest hospital and hoped for the best.

We may be dysfunctional, but we don't let people die in the hospital waiting room if we can help it, regardless of net worth. So usually, these people got decent care and a massive bill. Some worked out a payment plan, but others, especially the ones with bigger bills, ignored it or ducked out of it by declaring bankruptcy. The hospital then charged everybody else just a little more to make up for it, a situation that has always struck me as the perfect definition of socialized medicine.

So in the late 2000s, we finally decided to confront a system that guaranteed to everybody the most expensive form of hospital care available while not guaranteeing the sort of much cheaper primary and preventative care that might keep people out of that mess in the first place. Hence, the Affordable Care Act, a big hat-passing scheme for that 15 percent.

Basically, the law took that group of small business empresarios, their employees, tradesmen, bartenders, field workers, and poor wretches, and divided them into two groups. The poorest of the poor wretches were sent to newly expanded Medicaid, and everyone else got onto something that looked a lot like the old employer system, except the government was the H.R. department, in charge of recruiting insurance companies to come on down to an annual flea market called "open enrollment," where they could preen about wooing business – at least in theory.

The law solved the individual access problems described above by forcing insurance companies to sign up anybody whose money was green, regardless of health history. And before they could object on the basis that this would attract lots of sick people to the rolls and cause a quick trip to chapter 11, the government turned around and forced everyone to get insurance. This was supposed to guarantee that a certain number of healthy people would always be paying in and offsetting the sick people, something that has kind of almost worked, though not without some stiff premium increases.

But forcing people to get insurance is tough, and not just because of the legal challenge on that point that the law barely survived. First and foremost, not everybody can afford it, something employers traditionally solved by paying for most or all of it. With the ACA, The government solved that by setting up an elaborate sliding-scale financial aid system. (Heard about the tax credits/subsidies? That's it.)

Despite being reasonably clever, based as it was on a fully functioning state version pioneered by the known Marxist sympathizer Mitt Romney, the Affordable Care Act pleased approximately nobody at all. People who hate welfare programs hated it because it kind of smelled like one, rich small business owners notwithstanding. People who hated government spending of any kind hated it because it was government spending of a kind. Healthy affluent people with their act together hated it because instead of grooving out in an insurance group full of other healthy affluent people, they were now forced to buy insurance along with a lot of sick people, which was quite a bit more expensive. People of all political stripes hated that many plans came with family deductibles well over $10,000, meaning the insurance only really started after they paid that much ("free" birth control and flu shots exempted, naturally). And people who loved functioning websites also hated it for reasons you may have read about.

Conservatives, broadly speaking, hated it because it was yet another government entitlement that would be taken advantage of by a not-small number of people who do not pull their weight in society. They also hated the idea of the government forcing them to buy something, despite their long history with mandatory car insurance. They hated that the insurance package was so comprehensive that it included things they were unlikely to ever need, such as substance abuse treatment or maternity coverage (which men and non-addicts also paid for, because insurance could not possibly work any other way). And having been shielded from the true cost of insurance for decades by employers who just paid for it and moved on, they really hated to see the high cost of this stuff on the open market, especially if they had too much income for financial aid. (Somewhere out there, a wizened H.R. insurance professional read about that particular reaction, rolled their eyes, took a drag off an unfiltered cigarette, looked off into the distance, and quietly muttered, "welcome to my world.") Talk of government takeovers and socialized medicine ensued, as did allusions to the trampling on various freedoms.

Liberals, for their part, also hated the Affordable Care Act, mostly because it was not, as advertised by conservatives, a government takeover and socialized medicine. They also hated it because they loathe the insurance companies that played a big role in the new arrangement. Liberals tend to believe that medicine should not, fundamentally, be a for-profit proposition, and having big private companies buying healthcare on our behalf strikes them as crass at best and immoral at worst. (Even though the same thing happens all the time in those European countries they love talking about.) Probably feeding into this particular bit of hatred is the long history of insurance companies denying coverage to people with pre-existing health conditions (the medical equivalent of the drunk drivers), something they mistakenly blamed on the companies rather than the rules under which the companies had to operate.

Liberals for liberal reasons found the old situation and most of the new situation to be unconscionable. The ensuing loser talk would assert that any decently run society would see to the health of each of its citizens, regardless of ability to pay or whether they happen to work for a large company. They would then talk about healthcare being a human right, and perhaps share yet another anecdote about that vacation they took to Denmark, or some other country that guarantees free healthcare for all (and by "free" we mean they pay taxes instead of premiums). That's why, they say, we should shift everybody onto a "single payer" health plan organized by the government. Essentially, the feds would act as an insurance company, buying services on your behalf from private providers, just like in Canada and Taiwan. (The fact that the private providers in this arrangement worked for their own personal profit was apparently something they could overlook.)

Once again, we painted ourselves into the wimp corner on this one. Rallying to our side all the people who want to pass out free healthcare to send a message of national inclusiveness doesn't (quite obviously) get us a strong majority. The comparisons to foreign countries also lose Brownie points, because America is the best. And the sense of moral righteousness fences out all the people who would like a more sane system but don't wish to open their hearts to every hard luck medical case in a country of over 300 million people.

As a liberal for conservative reasons, I won't tell you that the system we have now is immoral. It is, however, stupid. Really, really, stupid. And hard to use. Check this out: The old system guaranteed that people who needed healthcare the most had the hardest time getting it, even if they had money. We denied people entry into insurance systems where they could have paid at least something, discouraged cheap primary care, then picked up the full tab when they ended up in the hospital and bankruptcy court. The Affordable Care Act fixed at least some of that, but still leaves us with a system that sentences Americans to a lifetime of bouncing around between health plans every time we move, change jobs, or change incomes (at age 34, I'm working on plan number ten).

That all means a ton of paperwork with lots of comparison shopping, deadline minding, tax form reading, and quite possibly new doctors to boot. I'm a political nerd with a college degree but each one of these handoffs still takes several hours of applied concentration – and that's before any actual claims have to be filed. It's easy to screw up, and it's still pretty expensive.

We used to have 50 million uninsured in the United States, and the Affordable Care Act cut that to 30 million or so. There are lots of reasons why that number is still quite high, despite everyone save illegal immigrants having some theoretical access, but one big reason is that getting insured is much more difficult than the cheaper option of throwing your hands up and doing nothing.

Should we care? Yes, but once again, not because of some humanistic guilt trip. We should care because if those uninsured people get into a fix, they revert to the old strategy, show up at a hospital, and we all end up paying for it. They will get a bill, a bankruptcy judge will tear up that bill, and the hospital will come back from court with a new plan to raise prices on the rest of us to make up for it. Clearly, we need to come up with a system where nobody gets to opt out like that. We also need something that's easy to use and better at negotiating down prices than the current crop of insurance companies.

(A brief word to my conservative friends who are thinking that perhaps we should quit treating people for free in hospitals, on the theory that this would motivate them into figuring something out. Most people think y'all are sick, sick puppies, but don't worry – your liberal friend Peter will listen. He's also willing to patiently tell you that while some people would indeed figure something out, on the whole this plan wouldn't work. First, "figuring something out" would often involve desperate phone calls to those in the extended family with their act together, and you can pretend to be going through a tunnel for only so long. Second, some people would actually die for lack of treatment, and while you may not personally care, you should care about the dependent children and elderly parents they leave behind becoming everybody's problem. Third, nothing galvanizes the takers quite like a bunch of people dying of fixable problems in first-world hospital waiting rooms. Take it from an occasional public relations professional: That stuff won't play well, and you will not enjoy the stiff political backlash. So just let's just keep that dark fantasy of yours on the down low, and I'll pretend this conversation never happened.)

Liberals, however, are out to lunch with this single payer nonsense. True, a single big government entity is a better price negotiator than a bunch of small insurance companies. And there may be some theoretical majority support for a single government insurance program paid for with taxes, but when people actually try to pass bills to that effect (Colorado, Vermont), the tax increases and general fear of massive change scare people off. Liberals, of course, correctly point out that the taxes add up to less than the premiums, and that it works great in Canada, but nobody likes math and we're not too sure about Canada either.

Liberals for conservative reasons will instead give people the option to voluntarily bail out of the present health insurance regime and buy their way into Medicare. There's a lot of talk in liberal circles about public options and state-based schemes, but we *already* have a wildly popular program that *already* has relationships with basically every doctor and hospital out there. They have, at the ready, enrollment forms, customer service reps, and a large staff capable of actually understanding the flurry of gobbledygook that doctors and hospitals mail you every time you take an aspirin in a medical facility.

Medicare is already decently inoculated against criticism, which is important in avoiding the normal fear of new or foreign things. Conservatives always seem to have at the ready a collection of shocking anecdotes about European systems that made someone wait in line for three months to get a box of Band-Aids or transplanted an eye onto someone's belly button by mistake. And these tales always struck me as pretty far fetched, but really, have I been to Finland? No, and who knows what they're capable of? And so it goes with arguments about foreign countries: The fear-based possibilities are endless.

So liberals can choose: Bring a knife to the gunfight and hope our nifty health outcome stats from the United Nations will make an impression on people's natural fear of the foreign unknown or a new program based on it, or just bring a gun and point out that old people in America seem to like American Medicare just fine, and there's no reason why American younger people wouldn't as well. Lots of people in their late 50s and early 60s are already there, and can't wait to get onto Medicare. Some people *are actually jealous of the disabled*, who are able to get on before age 65 ("Too bad about not being able to, you know, *walk*, but the health insurance ya got sure is terrific!"). So the big solution, instead of jumping into the single payer abyss, is to let individuals buy into Medicare at full price. That and saying "America" as much as possible.

(By now, some of you smartasses are probably yelling out that Medicare is a government-run single payer program, to which I would respond: Shut the hell up. This will just be our little secret over here, okay? Also while we're at it, never ever speak of a foreign country's health system in a positive light again. We cool? Good.)

As I was saying, let people buy into Medicare. Give the poor people some help buying in if they need it, just like we do now with private plans. Let businesses buy in for their employees if they feel like it, perhaps for a simple, flat percentage of payroll. Before too long, without any big tax increase or sudden mass-plan-migration freakout, basically everyone will be on Medicare, and we'll have taken a big bite out of that paperwork hassle and perennial doctor switching. Maybe you'll go from Medicare at your job to Medicare at your small startup, but Medicare can come up with internal procedures to make that seamless, which will lower the uninsured rate by reducing complication. Medicare could even merge its public face with Medicaid – so the bean counters in the back office will know which program you're really on, but you can keep the same card and not worry too much about getting kicked off when you suddenly make more than 138 percent of the poverty level. Eliminating that churn will also lower the uninsured rate.

Besides transferring all those obnoxious logistics from amateurs like us to professionals in Medicare offices, it'll even be cheaper, since Medicare can pretty well dictate terms to hospitals and doctors and generally encourage efficiency. They will dislike this, of course, just as they have disliked this since the creation of Medicare (for some good fun on your lunch break, put "Ronald Reagan speaks out against socialized medicine" into Youtube and see what pops up). They will continue to claim that they cannot possibly make a living on what Medicare pays, and then they will duck out to go meet with the ad agency that is presently putting up all those "Accepting New Medicare Patients!" billboards around town. We'll just let them blow off a little steam for a while and then move on with life. It may be that fewer doctors and hospital administrators have second homes under the new system, but I bet they scrape by anyway.

Liberals have been dreaming of a European-style universal healthcare system for decades. But raising taxes and forcing everyone out of private insurance all at once will never work, especially if the sales pitch involves divisive moralizing or, God forbid, actually talking about Europe. If they instead use a modified strategy with a conservative pitch – a voluntary buy in with more convenience, lower prices, no tax increases, and fewer freeloaders – there's at least a chance that one day soon, we can finally stop talking about this.

PETER RICE

Chapter Nine

The purity industrial complex, and how to never mention global warming.

ONE OF THE HIGHLIGHTS of my stint as a reporter in the extremely rural Oregon coastal hinterlands (described more in the trade chapter) was seeing firsthand just how much of normal life took place outside. The default option for recreation, either for a long weekend or the all-too-short window between the end of the workday and darkness, always revolved around some kind of hiking, fishing, camping, or other enticing outdoor pastime.

Nobody was immune. There was a lawyer downtown who always went fishing on his lunch break. The retired soil specialist who lived south of town had kept regular temperature and rain logs for years, and could identify seemingly every plant that might care to grow in a 100-mile radius. And there was a little cafe at the port that opened at 4 a.m. just for the fishing crowd. My publisher would write regular columns about hikes he took, and his weekend only really seemed to count if he was able to pick wild huckleberries and chanterelle mushrooms, which he would make into pancakes and various egg dishes, respectively. People would often walk into the paper without an appointment to drop off pictures of themselves posing with various fauna and marine life they had dispatched, and we happily printed them. We even let a group dedicated to protecting the local watershed meet in our basement conference room.

The vocabulary of nature permeated everything. Words like "steelie," "fingerling," "king," and "jack" needed no explanation and could be used in normal civilian conversation (fishing terms all). People even knew water measurement technique, and could easily explain the relevance of a "minus tide" while eyeballing a good guess at the "cfs" of the river. And we all knew going "upriver" to "the bar" was actually a BYOB affair.

These people, in short, basically lived outside, despite the Oregon coast's incessant rain. Many of them made their money outside. They took visiting friends outside to show them a good time. There was a deeper connection to the environment and the natural world there than any other bigger city I've been to, anywhere in the world. But if you asked, they would all have a few choice words for the people they viewed as public enemy number one: environmentalists.

The reason behind their all-encompassing hatred for these monsters is simple: It's the catch-all term for people who shrank the logging industry to a scale model of its former self, and were at the time working on the fishing business as well. But the larger questions the situation raises are more complicated and more interesting: How is it that a bunch of people who work in offices and commute to subdivisions every night, rarely leaving what planners call the "built environment," are the environmentalists? And even accepting that they are, how is it that they can't make common cause with the people that have three fishing trips on the calendar right now and consider that to be merely a good start?

The answer, I suspect, starts with nature documentaries watched by children. They usually feature some super cute herbivore just trying to make it out there in the big world (at least this was the formula back in the day when modern environmentalists were watching them). In the nature magazines I read as a kid, these cute things were even given names, personalities, and other anthropomorphic traits.

The programs slowly build up a snuggly, pastoral life for these furry protagonists, prominently featuring everything kids love. There was lots of playing around, often in water, and a strong omnipresent maternal figure to guide the babies along. And it was all in the woods, which fits right into children's natural tendency to play "pretend." Once the kiddos were putty in the producer's hands, one of two things happened: Either some predator came along and tore the cuteness limb from limb, or we saw footage of some dude with a chainsaw, then heard about how this bad man will eventually doom the cute.

It was the classic narrative of good and evil that kids are well accustomed to, but instead of the evil stepmother or dragon in the cave, we had bulldozers marauding over a strip mining operation (hard at work, no doubt, extracting material to make televisions for tomorrow's nature documentaries). From those narrative doldrums, they might try to round off this emotional hit job on some kind of high note, but the impression had long since been made. And thus we, at least those of us on team liberal, grow up thinking of the natural world as a temple of purity that the forces of evil violate because they care not for the innocent animals. Quite naturally, we all felt absolutely terrible about it. We were practically panicking about the state of the rainforest, the rivers, and the melting block of ice that the polar bear was standing on, and we needed something – anything – to do about it.

And here, the environmental movement told us, were some things you can do: Put these funny looking light bulbs up all over your house. And instead of throwing all of your household waste into one container, separate it out into these different containers for a magical process called recycling. And these plastic ring holders that keep six packs of soda together – be sure to cut those up so the baby otters don't get strangled to death. And for those who find all that too challenging, try to at least to not run the water *the entire time* you are brushing your teeth. Then say three Hail Marys and go and sin no more.

Many people did these things. As a young lad, I was in charge of the family recycling, and we were early adopters of those light bulbs. And while it probably didn't hurt anything, it dramatically failed to stop the unending barrage of nature documentaries with cute animals being led to the slaughter by dudes holding chainsaws.

By the late 1990s and early aughts, things had been duly kicked up a notch, with an even bigger list of things you could do to Save The Planet. There was shopping at Whole Foods, for example, where it was supposed that a four dollar tin can of corn with green leaves more prominently placed in the graphic design scheme was monumentally more sustainable than the $.68 (or two for $1) can at the normal grocery store. One could also buy a Prius, because all those batteries were presumably made out of baby farts and good vibes, rather than piles of toxic waste. You could also fill up your car at British Petroleum, which switched its logo from a shield to a sunburst, kicking off its "beyond petroleum" campaign by emphasizing its deep commitment to running ads about its deep commitment to alternative energy. (You may have heard about the tragic incident in 2010 in which 4.9 million barrels of solar panels and wind turbines spilled into the Gulf of Mexico.)

Again, none of these particular actions really made the situation worse, per se. But it didn't really seem to make it much better either.

Those damn nature documentaries kept coming, now supplemented by more serious global warming treatments featuring Al Gore and Leonardo DiCaprio.

All this, however, failed to impress rural conservatives who are out in nature so much that their houses seem purely decorative. They spent lifetimes mining coal, harvesting timber, farming crops, pumping oil, and generally busting the natural-world-as-temple-of-purity myth. They sold that stuff to liberals in big cities, only to later discover that their customers were ashamed of their purchases and had convinced themselves that if they didn't see it, it didn't really have any environmental impact – much like some people manage to believe that hamburgers have no relation to cows.

Eventually, environmentalists scared and guilted and smugged themselves into caring a lot about a problem much bigger than whatever would happen if we didn't separate the plastic and the aluminum: Global warming, the nerdiest mother of all environmental concerns. Basically, the carbon we all spew into the atmosphere by breathing, letting cows breathe, and burning stuff in engines becomes a total turkey of one-way blanket that lets in light from the sun, but does not let out the heat it generates – at least not fast enough.

Trouble was that, in the process of firing themselves up to take action, liberals had really annoyed everybody else. They asked conservatives nicely if they would be interested in, you know, *conserving* the atmosphere as we had come to know it. But by then, far too many of them had seen this obnoxious spectacle of environmentalist preening. Besides, lots of them couldn't actually afford a Prius, even if they would consent to be seen in one. If doing something about this global warming business meant in any way having to be like liberals, they seemed to reason, they were not interested. (And I can relate: If I am ever in a situation where I am totally unable to recycle an old soda can, I get a lovely little secret thrill knowing how much that situation would piss off environmentalists. Then I throw it away, sentence it to a landfill for all eternity, and smile to myself.) Add in that bothersome part about threatening people's jobs, and the lack of interest turned to hostility pretty quick.

So began the sort of rationalization that people always go through when they don't want to believe something supported by evidence, a mission made incredibly easy by the mechanics of the problem itself. It takes a pretty good imagination to picture that invisible one-way blanket. It's tough to get super excited about a couple degrees worth of temperature change when the average human in the average day experiences temperature changes much wilder than that. And not to sound like a total rube or member of Congress here, but *it still gets cold in the winter.* Is that a scientific assessment that you should take into account when deciding whether you "believe" in this stuff? Heavens no. But it sure is intuitive, and that's what liberals have chosen to fight against.

Get out into nature sometime. The woods, some tundra, a quiet beach – it doesn't matter. Take a few deep breaths. Observe the beauty, the vast expanse of the planet, and just how small a part of it we humans are at the end of the day, both now and in the 4 billion-year stretch of time this rock has been tooling around that star up there. Now think: we're burning so much stuff in our factories, airplanes, and cars that this could become, in the geological blink of an eye, a fiery hellscape.

That is, of course, a scientific consensus, but it seems totally fantastic. "Nah," you want to say, "it couldn't possibly do that. Little old us? We were celebrating the invention of stone tools, like, yesterday, and now we have that sort of power?" That, I suspect, is the conclusion of so many rural conservatives who so frequently find themselves out in nature. For city-dwelling environmentalists, nature is fragile. For rural conservatives who live and recreate outside, nature is tough and unrelenting. From that base, it's easy to conclude that a little carbon never hurt anybody.

Again, that's wrong, to the best of our knowledge. That majestic panorama could become Venus, if we're not careful, at least according to a bunch of smart people I've decided to trust. And I vote accordingly, but that doesn't make the notion any more believable.

It should surprise nobody, therefore, that a bunch of people take no stock in a totally counterintuitive, long-term, invisible problem proffered by the most annoying people ever to set foot in Whole Foods, and backed up by scientists in research institutions that are by design elite and aloof. And they appear to be after your job. Ever the sympathetic sort, liberals for liberal reasons label these people as science-denying neanderthals. And that goes over about as well as you would expect: Those who hear the slight are ticked off. The people of Curry County will also hear it and be ticked off, but it may take a while. That's because they're all out hunting, fishing, boating, camping, hiking, rafting, kayaking, surfing, mushroom hunting, and clamming, and will have put off the wholesale rejection of your *environmental message* until later.

The liberal-for-conservative-reasons solution to this mess is, thankfully, much simpler than the first draft: Skip the guilt trip, the conspicuous consumption, and the cute animals, and just talk about air pollution.

Air pollution is a great foundation to fight the good environmental fight. You can see it, for one thing: it comes out of tailpipes and smokestacks and accumulates over cities in depressing hazes. You can even smell it at close range. We've all felt a little sick in the stomach after getting too close to a cloud of diesel smoke coming out of tractor trailer, or felt a little funny in the throat the morning after a good campfire. Death by air pollution, in the form of a car and a well-sealed garage, is the plot of some movies and TV shows. We also know what smoking does to us, and to our clothes. And many people who live in the West have at one point been downwind of a wildfire, and they can all vouch for the ill effects. That makes it much harder for some group of "air pollution skeptics" to come along and tell you that the science is still not quite settled.

And while global warming's downside is hard to quantify and will play out over centuries, we know that air pollution causes about

200,000 premature deaths in the United States every year, according to one MIT study. As in, this year. (Worldwide, that number is well into the millions.) Know somebody who died of lung cancer even though they didn't smoke? Odds are decent they got bumped off by air pollution. It increases your risk of dying from a stroke and heart disease too, and causes or makes worse asthma.

From a public relations perspective, this is gold. The victims live all over the place and should be pretty easy for any two-bit reporter or citizen blogger to find. It touches every neighborhood regardless of median home price. Red states, blue states, even rural areas, since they're often close to those huge coal-fired power plants. Best of all, the people most likely to die are defenseless kids and the elderly, so it'll be tough to narc out of this problem by otherizing them as people we don't like. Also, old people vote at impressively high rates.

And how do we fight it? First, technology. This is where we can talk about wind and solar power, mileage standards, and electric cars, hopefully without the obnoxious elitist baggage from before. People basically love cool gadgets and infrastructure, and they'll even pay a little bit extra for it. Not to assuage your guilt over the penguins, of course, but try selling them on cleaner air and a longer life for grandma, and you might get somewhere.

Second strategy: Tax refunds. The carbon tax idea has been around for a long time, but lately it's gained traction with even some prominent conservatives, like Hank Paulson, James Baker, and George Schultz. The details can get complicated, but the basic idea is to tax every unit of carbon that is put into the economy. Like all taxes, it would discourage the thing being taxed and create all sorts of crazy tax evasion schemes, which in this case would involve large segments of American industry trying like crazy not to produce carbon. We would, of course, need to rename this plan the air pollution tax refund, but the effect would be the same.

And all that money generated? You get it all back in the form of a check. Some liberals might propose to spend that money promoting clean energy or some other predictable liberal cause like affordable housing or gender awareness classes for all, but they should resist. In the first place, there's no point in having two fights when you could only have one, and conservatives will want that money back. Secondly, while lots of voters could care less about whatever program you're going to finance with the money, you'll have to pry those refund checks from their cold, dead hands. It may even create a new constituency advocating draconian increases in the air pollution tax, and thus the refund. And if it works, you've got a great tool to fight other types of pollution.

The best part of a campaign against air pollution is that we can see the results and can actually win. The trouble with the proposed global warming solutions is that we don't know if they'll work, since, you know, *China still exists*. And even if they do, it'll be a while before we know. Maybe in 2100 we'll all have a rolicking champagne-soaked party celebrating how the overall global temperature only went up 1.5 degrees instead of 3, but my planner only goes through the end of 2017, and I'll be lucky to make it to 2070. An aggressive effort against air pollution could get some seriously visible results in just a few years, and everything we do would help the larger global warming cause.

Liberals are right to be concerned about global warming and carbon emissions, however annoying they've been about it, and they've mastered the very counterintuitive nature of the whole problem. So perhaps they'll be up for an incongruous strategy to actually win: Fight global warming by never speaking of it again.

PETER RICE

Epilogue

Why morality always belongs in politics, but sometimes should be seen and not heard.

I COULD GO ON, OF COURSE.

Immigration, healthcare, abortion, the environment, and trade are all marquee issues right now, but there are others as well. How legal should it be to get stoned, for example. And who can use which bathrooms - that sure seems to be animating quite a few people these days. The cops, meanwhile, do seem to shoot quite a few unarmed non-white people, don't they? What about North Korea, a country that could make all these issues suddenly seem very small? We're still fighting a war in Afghanistan, the national debt is still growing, we're all still way too fat, and the Middle East is still the Middle East.

On the lighter side, there is the deep and enduring mystery of Steve Bannon's face, and whether the greasy Bond villain look is cultivated or just comes naturally.

Like I said, I could go on. There are plenty more issues in the American canon. But I won't, because I think you've got the point. Perhaps liberals for liberal reasons could channel their outrage into another couple hundred pages, but liberals for conservative reasons will just keep things short and sweet and move on. As mentioned at the beginning, I have lots of conservative friends with nice patios, but I feel like I've been neglecting them and their generous pitchers of margaritas, what with all this writing.

Besides, this book wasn't really about issues. It was about one vision for the country and two strategies for getting there.

The liberal-for-liberal-reasons template is quite simple: Find an underdog to empathize with, ask what sinister governmental or corporate force can be blamed for the injustice, demonize everyone who doesn't totally agree, go camping somewhere to support the cause, and tell yourself you're right over and over again. Maybe, if you're feeling particularly chipper, organize a day without something or a privilege checking seminar with a focus on microaggressions. I hope I've convinced you that this is about as productive as recent elections would indicate.

The new template is just a new set of questions: What is the overall liberal goal? What are we actually trying to do in terms of legislation to make life a little more secure and bearable for normal people, especially the poor? What are the possible reasons for supporting action or reform in that direction? And most critically: Which of those reasons appeals to the widest possible audience?

Issues come and go, and the template won't work for all of them, but speaking the language of the opposition is never a bad way to sell your agenda. Liberals really enjoy being the change they want to see in the world, and they're basically quite good at it, but that's just talking to yourself. The trick to is to talk to others, then elect people that will legislate the change you want to see in the world.

But what's a liberal for liberal reasons to do with a template that seems to advocate for the abandonment of morality? For many decades now, for example, they have supported universal healthcare because it was the right and proper thing for decent modern societies to do. And there they were, more-or-less minding their own business, when some doofus came along to tell them to support it for the sake of convenience, and to make sure the freeloaders start paying up for a change. A double take in this situation would be quite normal.

And look at what we're up against, liberals may wonder. The opposition includes some scary characters, including open racists like Rep. Steve King and President "Textbook Definition of a Racist Comment." You want us to change our talking points and way of thinking to appeal to people who reckon voting for *that* is a good idea? It all seems so wrong, so crass. What happened to The Right Thing? Have you no sense of decency, sir? At long last, have you left no sense of decency?

Not to worry. The right thing isn't going anywhere, but it does not take away the necessity of accurately reading the electorate. Do that, and you'll find a lot of the despicable people you imagine when you think of conservatives, but you'll also find a lot of normal decent people you would be pleased to share a back fence with. You'll find people who voted for Barack and Bill. You'll find a lot of folks who are easy to work with all day and fun to hang out with at night. Really, they're just like Muslims: They have some strange and completely unprovable ideas, but when you get to meet them in person, they seem pretty friendly and accommodating about the whole thing. Except for the jerks, but luckily there aren't too many of them. Kind of reminds me of Christians, come to think of it. And vegetarians. And Rotarians. And Democrats. And humans.

Getting where we want to go with conservatives doesn't mean winning over the vigilante militia types who dress up in camo and patrol the border in their all-too-abundant spare time. We just need to carve off a few of the more reasonable ones and we'll be fine. After all, if Hillary had bumped up her totals in three key states by a measly two percentage points, she would be president right now. Five percentage points nationwide, and we'd be talking about the leftist landslide, possibly involving victories in Arizona and North Carolina.

This is not to say that morality-based arguments have never worked and never will. After all, we just finished winning the gay marriage wars by hyping simple full equality for all, hardly a liberal-for-conservative-reasons argument. An army of normal, wonderful, appealing people came out of the closet and forced everyone else to make an emotional, moral choice between them and the stone age thoughts in their head. And then we won, which sure felt pretty good.

The liberal-for-conservative-reasons argument for gay marriage would have gone something like this: The state's interest in marriage has nothing to do with love or deep emotional commitments or anybody's religious tradition. It's two people forming a small corporation and entering into a series of contracts that spell out who gets the stuff and who takes care of the kids if you break up. The goal is just to avoid protracted legal fights and nasty surprises. So of course gay people should be included, because otherwise we'll just clog up the courts and waste everybody's money.

Not very satisfying, was it? Sure it makes sense, from an emotionless technical point of view that Mr. Spock would doubtless approve of. But does it feel good? Hardly.

I understand the attraction to moral arguments – really. And I use them myself frequently, because they're so simple. On the subject of murder, for example, I'm fine with saying it's wrong and calling it a day. There's no need to talk about the impact legalized murder would have on business, or to wax on about how it would be wasteful for society to dump so much money into educating children only to have them bumped off at random. We just don't need to go there.

The key is to distinguish between issues that are settled (murder), issues that are winnable (gay marriage), and issues that are going to need a bigger tent to become settled (everything else in this book). We can ignore the settled stuff and press on with simple moral arguments where the demographic wind is at our backs, but we need to recognize what issues need wider appeal and adjust our thinking accordingly.

If this concept seems a tad familiar, that's because you may have, once upon a time, read the Just War Doctrine, the Catholic Church's take on the perennial moral quandary of when to take up arms and when to stay home. It's basically a checklist of legitimacy. Did you exhaust every other option, it asks? Also: Do people have a right to depose the government waging the war? And most interesting of all: Is there a reasonably good chance of success?

We've known for a long time that fighting a war for a cause you can't win is a bad idea. Lots of people will die and no good will come of it. No matter how just the cause, creating a lot of carnage won't help unless you win in the process.

Politics, they say, is just war by other means, and while it leaves fewer dead bodies strewn across the landscape, it still hurts people and often damages or destroys carefully cultivated relationships. During the gay marriage fight, lots of conservatives felt personally attacked. They got angry, and probably took out that frustration on others or on other issues we care about. They felt isolated as well, which is a risky business for a social species in a country with universal adult suffrage. Start a fight, and there's no telling where it will end. Massive controversies bring high tensions, accusations of racism, dismissals of entire populations as ignorant rubes, and retreats into tribal corners. The fog of war by other means is still fraught with peril.

With same-sex marriage, the cause was just, but fighting for it left a few metaphorical bodies out on the field. It was not free of negative consequences, but in the end, we won and it's settled. The new president couldn't care less, the right will be secure in perpetuity, and our union is a little more perfect because of it.

Liberals go out and fight every day for their just causes – for women, for the poor, for the giant panda, for whatever. But without a reasonably good chance of success, all we get for our weaponized sanctimony are consequences without victories. Morality, a longing for justice, and a respect for the inherent worth and dignity of every person are the basis of liberalism for any reason at all. But liberals for conservative reasons believe that our obligations to the weakest among us include an obligation to win.

PETER RICE

Acknowledgements

Many thanks to the crack editing team, including Andrew Clouse, David Dobbs, Brian Loftus, Dave Bellefeuille-Rice, and Judith Rios Duarte. And a special thanks to chief consigliere, Lindsay Wood. Without your time and patience, this book would not have been possible. Actually, that's not true. But it would have sucked pretty bad.

About the author

Peter Rice is a journalist and writer based in Albuquerque, New Mexico. He has covered local and state politics there, as well as in Oregon and Washington, for a variety of newspapers and radio stations. He is the author of the decidedly non-political *Spandex Optional Bicycle Touring: How to ride long distance, the cheap and easy way*, which is available on Amazon. He would love to hear from you through the contact section at peterbrice.com.

Made in the USA
Columbia, SC
07 June 2017